Vüe du Nouveau Palais près de la porte triomphale
d'Anitschki vers l'orient avec une partie de la ville & du chemin
du Monastere d'Alexandre Newski prise du Coté de la Fontanka.

EIGHTEENTH-CENTURY

RUSSIAN BIBLIOGRAPHY

A.G. CROSS   G.S. SMITH

Eighteenth Century Russian Literature Culture and Thought: A Bibliography of English—Language Scholarship and Translations

Oriental Research Partners, Newtonville, 1984

Manufactured in the United States of America

Library of Congress card number: 84-060143

Cross, Anthony Glenn; Smith, Gerald Stanton
Eighteenth-Century Russian Literature, Culture and Thought:
A Bibliography of English-language Scholarship and
Translations

ISBN 0-89250-334-3

Светлой памяти
академика
Михаила Павловича Алексеева
1896–1981

CONTENTS

(Personalia, continued)

ACKNOWLEDGEMENTS

We would like to thank once again the friends and colleagues who have helped us in our bibliographical labours over the years, especially Dr R.P. Bartlett, Dr P. Dukes, Dr J. Dunstan, Dr L.A.J. Hughes, Mr J.S.G. Simmons, and Mr G. Terry.

We are especially grateful to Mr I.C.S. Smith for compiling the chronological indexes and making a substantial contribution to the other indexes.

The fundamental editorial work on this volume was carried out during Dr G.S. Smith's tenure of a Research Fellowship in the University of Liverpool; he would like to thank this institution, and also Mrs Joan Stevenson of the Department of Russian, for their support and help.

We are also grateful to the Department of Slavonic Studies, University of British Columbia, for the kind provision of facilities.

The dedication of this book acknowledges a personal debt on both our parts to the greatest Russian scholar in the field with which it is concerned. We were privileged to know him for many years, and that he did not survive to perch this volume on his overflowing desk is a matter of great regret to both of us.

A.G.C., G.S.S.

September,1983

INTRODUCTION

   This book brings together and updates the bibliographies that
the authors have been publishing together at intervals since 1976,
and adds to them a bibliography of translations into English of
eighteenth-century Russian literary works.

   Our compilation is intended principally as a practical tool for
those engaged in, or contemplating, research into the subject areas
indicated in the title. But it has in addition an important
subsidiary purpose. This is to provide the materials towards a
history of the study of eighteenth-century Russian culture in the
English-speaking world. It is for this reason that the entries are
arranged, within the broad subject headings, in chronological order,
and chronological lists of both translations and secondary works have
been furnished among the appendixes.

   The core of the Bibliography is formed by the information it
provides about literary translation and the study of literary history.
To arrive at hard and fast definitions of the subject areas beyond
literature has been a constant problem. We have been aware that our
work complements, but also overlaps with, the work of Bartlett and
Clendenning in this same series; given the existence of their book,
we have felt free to draw our boundaries restrictively rather than
generously in certain areas.

   We have, however, excluded from our listings certain kinds of
publication that certainly fall within the central core of our
subject, and we are fully aware that our list is by no means
exhaustive. Most importantly, we have left aside all but a very few
reviews. Those reviews that have been included have found a place
either because of their pioneering historical importance, or, in more
modern times, because we have felt that the reviewer supplies
important information that cannot be discovered elsewhere within our
listings. Another category of publication that we have excluded, in
some cases with considerable regret, is formed by the synopses of
papers delivered to the Study Group on Eighteenth-Century Russia
published in the Group's annual Newsletter. The recent appearance of
an Index to the Newsletter that includes these synopses as well as
many substantial reviews, however, has tempered our regret: J.Sherrif,
R.Lucas, 'Index to the Newsletter Nos 1-10, 1973-82', Study Group on
Eighteenth-Century Russia Newsletter, 10(1982), 75-103.

   We have made no attempt to provide full bibliographical
descriptions of books, but have restricted our data to the place and
date of publication.

   Within the general rubric "eighteenth-century" we have been
flexible in drawing chronological boundaries. We have, for example,
taken our coverage of the work of Derzhavin, Dmitriev, Kapnist and
Karamzin right up to their deaths, which all occurred after 1815, but
we have omitted coverage of Krylov the fabulist on the grounds that

this phase of his career is a nineteenth-century phenomenon. We beg the indulgence of our readers and their undoubted awareness of the problems besetting the periodisation of the subject.

We have had considerable difficulties in many cases with the assigning of items to one of our subject categories rather than another; having decided in principle against making duplicate entries, we became even more aware of the arbitrary element in some of our decisions. We hope that the relative fullness of the indexation will overcome this arbitrariness. Perhaps the most important warning to make in this respect is that we have tended to over-assign the earlier publications to the "General Histories" category rather than burying them in the body of the "Personalia" as their contents would sometimes seem to require. We have acted in this way in order to amplify the historical sequentiality of the "General" category.

The Bibliography was prepared for the press in May, 1983, and entries were being incorporated into the body of the work until the beginning of that month. We felt it proper to include the contents of one major collection which was unpublished at the time of closing compilation: this is the special issue of Russian Literature Triquarterly that is to appear as Nos 20/21 of that journal, edited by the present writers. It was delivered to the publisher in the autumn of 1979. With some regret, we have only been able to list among the Addenda the relevant items from another major collection, the Proceedings of the International Conference on Russia and the West in the Eighteenth Century, held in Norwich, U.K., in 1981 and edited by Professor A.G. Cross; this volume was published only after the basic text of the Bibliography and the indexes had been finished.

Our individual contributions to this publication have not been uniform. After our initial pooling of card indexes in 1974, the accumulation of source material, especially the older translations, has principally been the concern of A.G. Cross; the arrangement, editing, and preparation for the press has been mainly the work of G.S. Smith. However, we take full joint responsibility for the merits and demerits of the result. We hope that it will inspire parallel publications dealing with the contributions of other non Russian-speaking countries to this particular area of scholarly enquiry and eventually form one element in an international research effort.

ARRANGEMENT OF THE BIBLIOGRAPHY

As indicated in the list of contents, the Bibliography is divided into fourteen principal categories according to subject matter. Four of these categories have been sub-divided. Categories A, B, and G have three, two, and six sub-categories respectively. Category N, "Personalia", contains individual entries for seventy-five authors and another for anonymous works. An author has been assigned an individual sub-category if even a single separately published translation or scholarly work has been wholly devoted to him or her. Category N is arranged in alphabetical order according to the transliteration of the author's surname.

Within these categories and sub-categories, entries are set out in chronological order of publication by year. If there are multiple entries for a single year, they are arranged in alphabetical order according to the surname of the author. Where appropriate, however, collections have been placed first in the series of entries for the year in which they appeared.

Within the entries for individual authors, translations precede secondary works. The translations are listed in alphabetical order according to the transliteration of their title in Russian. The category "O.N.E." ("Original Not Established"), bringing together works whose original we have not been able to ascertain, is placed at the end of the list of translations for the author concerned. Anonymous works are listed under the rubric "Anonymous" at the appropriate alphabetical place in Category N.

Where no translator is named as such, the translation is as a rule to be ascribed to the editor or compiler of the collection in which the translation was published.

The dates in parenthesis after the transliterated titles of literary works are those of composition unless otherwise indicated.

Translations of works written in languages other than Russian by Russian authors have been included alongside translations of works written in Russian.

Dissertations have not been listed if their contents have been fully published in another form.

All items in the Bibliography have been described de visu, with the exception of some dissertations submitted to universities outside the United Kingdom, and two entries (Nos. 29 and 30) marked with an asterisk.

The place of publication of books is London unless otherwise indicated.

ABBREVIATIONS

Collections

Black	Essays on Karamzin: Russian Man-of-Letters, Political Thinker, Historian, 1766-1826, edited by J.L. BLACK (The Hague-Paris, 1975). (No.873)
Bowring	BOWRING, J., Specimens of the Russian Poets. With Preliminary Remarks and Biographical Notices (2 vols, 1821-3). (No.25)
Brown	BROWN, W.E., A History of 18th Century Russian Literature (Ann Arbor, 1980) (No.94)
Cross	Russian Literature in the Age of Catherine the Great, edited by A.G. CROSS (Oxford, 1976) (No.86)
Dukes	Russia under Catherine the Great, edited by P. DUKES (2 vols, Newtonville, 1977). I, Select Documents on Government and Society; II, Catherine the Great's Instructions (NAKAZ) to the Legislative Commission, 1767
Garrard	The Eighteenth Century in Russia, edited by J.G. GARRARD (Oxford, 1973) (No.83)
GBR	Great Britain and Russia in the Eighteenth Century: Contacts and Comparisons, edited by A.G. CROSS (Newtonville, 1979) (No.203)
Lewis	LEWIS, W.D., The Bakchesarian Fountain. By Alexander Pooshkeen. And Other Poems, By Various Authors, Translated from the Original Russian (Philadelphia, 1849) (No.26)
Nebel	Selected Prose of N.M. Karamzin, edited and with an Introduction by H.M. NEBEL, jr (Evanston, 1969) (No.758)
PRR	GUERNEY, B.G., The Portable Russian Reader. A Collection Newly Translated from Classical and Present-Day Authors (New York, 1947) (No.34)
RLT,20/21	Russian Literature Triquarterly, Nos 20/21 (Special Issue on the Eighteenth Century, edited by A.G. CROSS and G.S. SMITH) (In Press)
Segel	SEGEL, H.B., The Literature of Eighteenth-Century Russia, 2 vols (New York, 1967) (No.22)
TRL	GUERNEY, B.G., A Treasury of Russian Literature (New York, 1943; London, 1948) (No.33)
Wiener	WIENER, L., Anthology of Russian Literature, 2 vols (New York and London, 1902-3) (No.28)

Journals

| CSP | Canadian Slavonic Papers |

CSS   Canadian-American Slavic Studies (formerly Canadian Slavic Studies)

HSS   Harvard Slavic Studies

HT   History Today

MLR   Modern Language Review

MSlS   Melbourne Slavonic Studies

OSP   Oxford Slavonic Papers

RR   Russian Review

SEEJ   Slavic and East European Journal

SEER   Slavonic and East European Review (formerly Slavonic Review)

SGECRN   Study Group on Eighteenth-Century Russia Newsletter

SR   Slavic Review

EIGHTEENTH-CENTURY RUSSIAN

LITERATURE, CULTURE AND THOUGHT:

A BIBLIOGRAPHY OF

ENGLISH-LANGUAGE

SCHOLARSHIP AND TRANSLATIONS

A. BIBLIOGRAPHY

i. Library Holdings

1. FESSENKO, T., Eighteenth-Century Publications in the Library of Congress: A Catalog (Washington, 1961).

2. TYRRELL, E.P., and SIMMONS, J.S.G., 'Slavonic Books of the Eighteenth Century in Cambridge Libraries', Transactions of the Cambridge Bibliographical Society, IV, 3(1966), 225-45.

3. KASINEC, E., 'Eighteenth-Century Russian Publications in the New York Public Library. A Preliminary Catalog. Parts I-II', Bulletin of the New York Public Library, LXXI, 9(1969), 599-614; LXXV, 9(1971), 474-94.

4. DRAGE, C.L., 'Eighteenth-Century Church Slavonic and Russian Books in United Kingdom Libraries', Solanus, 13(1978), 1-13.

5. DRAGE, C.L., and SCREEN, J.O., 'Church Slavonic and Russian Books (1552-1800) in the Library of the School of Slavonic and East European Studies', SEER, 57, 3(1979), 321-47.

ii. Subject Bibliographies

6. LINE, M.B., A Bibliography of Russian Literature in English Translation, to 1900 (1963).

7. LEWANSKI, R.C., The Literatures of the World in English Translation. A Bibliography. II: The Slavic Literatures (New York, 1967).

8. TURKEVICH, I., Spanish Literature in Russia and in the Soviet Union (1735-1964) (Metuchen, N.J., 1967).

9. NERHOOD, H.W., To Russia and Return: An Annotated Bibliography of Travelers' English-Language Accounts of Russia from the Ninth Century to the Present (Columbus, Ohio, 1968).

10. CROWTHER, P.A., A Bibliography of Works in English on Early Russian History to 1800 (Oxford, 1969).

1

11. SMITH, G.S., 'A Select Bibliography of Works on Eighteenth-Century Russian Versification Published Outside the Soviet Union', SGECRN, 1(1973), 43-8.

12. TERRY, G.M., East European Languages and Literatures. A Subject and Name Index to Articles in English-Language Journals, 1900-1917 (Oxford and Santa Barbara, 1979).

13. BARTLETT, R.P., and CLENDENNING, P., Eighteenth-Century Russia: A Select Bibliography of Works Published since 1955 (Newtonville, 1981). Section 12, 'Intellectual History and Culture'; Section 11, 'Individuals, Biographies and Culture'.

14. TERRY, G.M., East European Languages and Literatures II. A Subject and Name Index to Articles in Festschriften, Conference Proceedings, and Collected Papers in the English Language, 1900-1981, and Including Articles in Journals, 1978-1981 (Nottingham, 1982).

iii. Current Bibliography

15. American Bibliography of Russian and East European Studies (Bloomington, 1956-).

16. 'Russian Studies: The Eighteenth Century', in The Year's Work in Modern Language Studies; by C.A.JOHNSON (1963-1976, Cambridge, 1964-1977); by L.A.J.HUGHES (1977- , Cambridge, 1978-).

17. CROSS, A.G., and SMITH, G.S., 'A Bibliography of English-Language Scholarship on Eighteenth-Century Russian Literature, Thought and Culture (1900-1974), in Cross, 195-217.

18. CROSS, A.G., and SMITH, G.S., 'A Bibliography of English-Language Scholarship on Eighteenth-Century Russian Literature, Thought and Culture since 1974', SGECRN, 5(1977), 55-65.

19. CROSS, A.G., and SMITH, G.S., 'A Bibliography of English-Language Scholarship on Eighteenth-Century Russian Literature, Thought and Culture since 1977', SGECRN, 7(1979), 47-58.

20. CROSS, A.G., and SMITH, G.S., 'A Bibliography of English-Language Scholarship on Eighteenth-Century Russian Literature, Thought and Culture since 1979', SGECRN, 9(1981), 57-67.

B. ANTHOLOGIES

i. Eighteenth-Century Texts

21. MANNING, C.A., _Anthology of Eighteenth Century Russian Literature_, 2 vols (New York, 1951).
    (Texts in Russian, with biographical notes in English).

22. SEGEL, H.B., _The Literature of Eighteenth-Century Russia_, 2 vols (New York, 1967).
    (Texts in English, with introductory article (see No.80 below), biographical notes, and bibliography). Review: Edgerton, W.D., 'Recent Anthologies of Eighteenth-Century Russian Literature: A Review Article', _SEEJ_, XII, 1(1968), 59-78.

23. DRAGE, C.L., and VICKERY, W.N., _An XVIIIth Century Russian Reader_ (Oxford, 1969).
    (Texts in Russian, with introductory article, biographical notes, textual commentaries).

ii. General

24. [BERESFORD, BENJAMIN, translator], _The Russian Troubadour or Collection of Ukrainian, and Other national Melodies, Together with the Words of each Respective Air translated into English Verse by the Author of the German Erato, Interspersed with several favourite Russian Songs, Set to Music by Foreign Masters, and Translated by the Same Hand_ (1816).

25. BOWRING, J., _Specimens of the Russian Poets. With Preliminary Remarks and Biographical Notices_, 2 vols (1821-3). There was a second edition, with additions, of Vol.I.(1821).

26. LEWIS, W.D., _The Bakchesarian Fountain. By Alexander Pooshkeen. And Other Poems, By Various Authors, Translated from the Original Russian_ (Philadelphia, 1849).

27. WILSON, C.T., _Russian Lyrics in English Verse_ (1887).

28. WIENER, L., _Anthology of Russian Literature_, 2 vols (New York and London, 1902-3); Reprinted, New York, 1967.
    (Vol.I is devoted to the eighteenth century; Vol.II includes Karamzin).

29. *HAPGOOD, I.F., _Survey of Russian Literature, with Selections_ (New York, 1902).

30. *PARR, M.S.L., _God and Other Poems, Translated by John Bowring_ (Boston, Mass., 1912).

31. RUDZINSKY, B.A., and GARDINER, S., Selections of Russian Poetry.
    Introduction by Donald MacAlister (Glasgow, 1918).
    Another, identical, edition: Poems selected from Karamzin,
    Pushkin, Tyutchev, Lermontov, Count A.Tolstoy, Nikitin,
    Pleshcheyev, Nadson and Sologub (Alya, London, Edinburgh,
    Glasgow, n.d.(1918).

32. COXWELL, C.F., Russian Poems, Translated with Notes.
    Introduction by D.Mirsky (1929).

33. GUERNEY, B.G., A Treasury of Russian Literature (New York, 1943;
    London, 1948).

34. GUERNEY, B.G., The Portable Russian Reader. A Collection Newly
    Translated from Classical and Present-Day Authors (New York,
    1947).
    (With foreword and biographical notes).

35. BOWRA, C.M., A Second Book of Russian Verse (1948).

36. YARMOLINSKY, A., A Treasury of Russian Verse (New York, 1949).

37. RAEFF, M., Russian Intellectual History: An Anthology. With an
    Introduction by Isaiah Berlin (New York, 1966).

38. RAFFEL, B., Russian Poetry under the Tsars (Albany, 1971).

39. VERNADSKY, G., FISHER, R.T., FERGUSON, A.D., LOSSKY, A., and
    PUSHKAREV, S., A Source Book for Russian History from Early
    Times to 1917. Vol II, Peter the Great to Nicholas I (New Haven
    and London, 1972).

C. GENERAL HISTORIES

40. HANWAY, J., Historical Account of the British Trade over the Caspian Sea, I (1753).
(Pp. 372-3 deal with the state of learning and contain some remarks about poetry).

41. [MACARTNEY, G.], Account of Russia, MDCCLXVII (1768).
('Of Arts and Sciences', pp.164-9, deals with the language and poetry, naming Lomonosov and Sumarokov).

42. CHAPPE D'AUTEROCHE, J., A Journey into Siberia, Made by Order of the King of France (1770).
('Of the Progress of the Arts and Sciences in Russia', pp. 319-23).

43. HARRIS, J., 'Account of Literature in Russia, and of its Progress towards being civilized', in his Philological Inquiries, II (1781).
Reprinted in Annual Register, Or a View of the History, Politics, and Literature, for the Year 1781 (1782), 158-63.

44. COXE, W., Travels into Poland, Russia, Sweden, and Denmark, II (1784).
(Chapter VIII contains a survey of Russian poetry and theatre, based largely on German (Bachmeister) and French (Le Clerc) sources.

45. ANON., articles in New and General Biographical Dictionary, 12 vols (1784).
(Includes biographies, based on materials in Coxe (No.44), of Kantemir, Kheraskov, Khilkov, Lomonosov, Shcherbatov, Sumarokov, Tatishchev, Prokopovich, and Volkov).

46. SWINTON, A., Travels into Norway, Denmark and Russia in the Years 1788, 1789, 1790 and 1791 (1792)
(Pp. 232-5 discuss Russian theatre and poetry, mentioning Lomonosov and Sumarokov).

47. CHANTREAU, P.N., Philosophical, Political, and Literary Travels in Russia, During the Years 1788 and 1789 (Perth, 1794).
(Armchair traveller's account, translated from French; chapters 18-19 discuss literature, based on Coxe (No.44) and Le Clerc.

48. ANON., 'Foreign Literature of the Year 1799', in The Annual Register or General Repository of History, Politics, and Literature for the Year 1799 (1800), 278-9.
(Mentions Karamzin, Kheraskov and others).

49. ANON., 'Russian Literature. Extract of a Letter from Moscow, 2nd of March, 1800', The Monthly Magazine; or British Register, X(1800), 51-3.
(On various Russian authors, especially Karamzin).

50. TOOKE, W., History of Russia from the Foundation of the Monarchy to the Accession of Catherine the Great, II (1800). (Pp. 404-18 deal with Moscow literature and theatre, especially Karamzin; pp. 472-6 contain a synopsis of Fonvizin's Nedorosl'. Adapted from J.RICHTER, Moskwa: eine Skizze (1799).)

51. STORCH, H., The Picture of Petersburg (1801). [Translated by William Tooke.] Pp. 293-458 contain a review of eighteenth-century Russian literature; this chapter was included, without acknowledgement of source, in Tooke's Life of Catharine II (3rd edition, 1799), III, 394-439.

52. ANON., Untitled review, The Edinburgh Magazine, or Literary Miscellany, NS XXII(October 1803), 147. (The present state of Russian letters). Reprinted in The Monthly Magazine; or British Register, XVI, 2(1803), 56.

53. ANON., Review of J.RICHTER, Russische Miszellen (1804), The Anti-Jacobin, XVIII(1804), 483-4. (The present state of Russian letters).

54. "A SURGEON IN THE BRITISH NAVY", A Voyage to St.Petersburg in 1814 (1822). (Pp. 64-5 discuss Sumarokov, Lomonosov, and Karamzin).

55. [BOWRING, J.], 'Politics and Literature in Russia', The Westminster Review, I, 1(April 1824), 80-101. (Lomonosov, Trediakovsky, Popovsky, Bogdanovich, Fonvizin, Khemnitser, Kapnist, Kostrov, Derzhavin, Karamzin, Bobrov, and Shishkov; based on Bestuzhev-Marlinskii's survey article in Poliarnaia zvezda, 1823).

56. [COCHRANE, J.G., and SMIRNOV, I.Ia.], Review of DUPRÉ DE SAINT MAURE, Anthologie russe, suivie de poésies originales (Paris, 1823), Foreign and Quarterly Review, I(1827), 595-628. (Pp. 609-21 survey eighteenth-century Russian literature).

57. GRANVILLE, A.B., St Petersburgh. A Journal of Travels to and from that Capital, II (1829). (Pp. 243-5, 'Russian Literature', mention Sumarokov, Khemnitser, Lomonosov, Karamzin, Murav'ev, and Krylov).

58. [LEEDS, W.H.], Essays in The Penny Cyclopaedia of the Society for the Diffusion of Useful Knowledge, 27 vols, 1833-43. (The essay on Russian language and literature in Vol.22 discusses eighteenth-century Russian literature in general; there are individual entries on Derzhavin (vol.8); Dmitriev (Vol.9); Kantemir, Kheraskov, Karamzin, Khemnitser (Vol.13); Lomonosov (Vol.15); Sumarokov (Vol.23); and Volkov (Vol.23).

59. BREMNER, R., Excursions into the Interior of Russia, I (1839). (Pp. 279-83, 'Russian Poets and Writers', mentions Bogdanovich, Dmitriev, Kantemir, Lomonosov, Kheraskov, Maikov, Kniazhnin, Kostrov, Fonvizin, Murav'ev, Derzhavin, Bobrov, and Karamzin).

60. OTTO, F., History of Russian Literature, with a Lexicon of
    Russian Authors (Oxford, 1839).
    (Translated by George Cox from Lehrbuch der russischen
    Literatur (Leipzig and Riga, 1837). Pp. 48-85 contain a survey
    of eighteenth-century Russian literature).

61. [LEEDS, W.H.?], 'Recent Literature in Russia', Foreign
    Quarterly Review, XXX(October 1842), 242-52.

62. GOLOVIN, I., Russia under the Autocrat Nicholas the First, II
    (1846).
    (Pp. 232-85, 'Of Russian Literature', mentions eighteenth-
    century poets (246-7) and Karamzin (234-40)).

63. [HENNINGSEN, C.F.], Eastern Europe and the Emperor Nicholas,
    II(1846).
    (Pp. 146-7 discuss Lomonosov, Derzhavin and Karamzin).

64. ANON., 'National Literatures. II. Russia', The Labourer, III
    (1848), 130-1.
    (Lomonosov, Derzhavin, Karamzin, Krylov).

65. TALVI (pseudonym of THERESA ALBERTINE LUISE VON JACOB,
    afterwards ROBINSON), Historical View of the Languages and
    Literature of the Slavic Nations: with a Sketch of their
    Popular Poetry (New York, 1850).
    (Pp. 60-79 deal with eighteenth-century Russian literature.)
    Originally published as 'Historical View of the Slavic
    Language in its various Dialects: with special reference to
    Theological Literature', Biblical Repository, IV, 14(April
    1834), 328-413; IV, 15(July 1834), 417-532, 615-16; and 'Slavic
    Popular Poetry', North American Review, XLIII(July 1836),
    85-120.

66. GRAHAME, F.R., The Progress of Science, Art, and Literature in
    Russia (1865).
    (Pp. 17-227 deal with eighteenth-century Russian literature up
    to Karamzin; Lomonosov, Derzhavin, Kapnist and Khemnitser are
    quoted in Bowring's translations).

67. TURNER, C.E., Studies in Russian Literature (1882).
    (Includes translated extracts from Lomonosov, Kantemir,
    Catherine II, Sumarokov, Fonvizin, Derzhavin, Krylov; pp. 1-115
    were previously published in Fraser's Magazine. See Nos. 516,
    621, 710, 732, 841, 1230).

68. MORFILL, W.R., Russia (1890).
    ('Catherine and the Arts', pp. 244-6).

69. GAUSSEN, W.F.A., Memorials of a Short Life. A Biographical
    Sketch of W.F.A.Gaussen, with Essays on Russian Life and
    Literature, edited by G.F.Browne (1895).
    ('Russian People and their Literature', pp.133-5).

70. WOLKONSKY, (PRINCE S.), Pictures of Russian History and Russian Literature (Boston, New York and London, 1897). (Lectures 5 and 6, pp. 129-80, deal with Russian literature from Lomonosov to Karamzin).

71. WALISZEWSKI, K., A History of Russian Literature (1900). (Pp. 47-147 cover the eighteenth century).

72. KROPOTKIN, P., Russian Literature: Ideals and Realities (1905; revised edition, 1916). (Chapter I, pp. 1-39; from the beginnings to the Decembrists).

73. BRUCKNER, A., A Literary History of Russia, translated by H. Havelock (London and Leipzig, 1908). (Pp. 60-138: "Transformed" Russia; Catherine II and her Time).

74. SHAKHNOVSKI, A Short History of Russian Literature, translated by Serge Tomkeyeff (1921). (Pp. 36-73).

75. MIRSKY, D.S., A History of Russian Literature. From the Earliest Times to the Death of Dostoyevsky (1881) (1927). (Pp.45-94; reprinted in D.S.MIRSKY, A History of Russian Literature. Edited and Abridged by Francis J.Whitfield (1949)).

76. HARKINS, W.E., Dictionary of Russian Literature (New York, 1956). (Includes entries on authors, genres, and literary movements).

77. ČIŽEVSKIJ, D., History of Russian Literature: From the Eleventh Century to the End of the Baroque (The Hague, 1962). (Pp. 382-438).

78. SLONIM, M., The Epic of Russian Literature. From its Origins Through Tolstoy (New York, 1964). (Pp. 29-54).

79. BILLINGTON, J.H., The Icon and the Axe: An Interpretive History of Russian Culture (1966). (Pp. 180-306).

80. SEGEL, H.B., 'Introduction', in The Literature of Eighteenth-Century Russia (New York, 1967), I, 25-116.

81. ČIŽEVSKIJ, D., Comparative History of Slavic Literatures (Vanderbilt, 1971). (Pp. 88-117).

82. CROSS, A.G., 'The Russian Literary Scene in the Reign of Paul I', CSS, VII, 1(1973), 39-51.

83. The Eighteenth Century in Russia, edited by J.G. GARRARD (Oxford, 1973).

8

84. GARRARD, J.G., 'Introduction: The Emergence of Modern Russian Literature and Thought', in Garrard, 1-21.

85. CURTISS, M., A Forgotten Empress: Anna Ivanovna and her Era (New York, 1974).
(Pp. 203-66, 'Opera and Ballet'; pp. 217-30, 'Science and Culture').

86. Russian Literature in the Age of Catherine the Great, edited by A.G.CROSS (Oxford, 1976).

87. CROSS, A.G., 'Russian Literature in the Reign of Catherine: Synchronic Tables', in Cross, 186-93

88. The Modern Encyclopedia of Russian and Soviet History, edited by J.L. WIECZYNSKI (Gulf Breeze, 1976-).

89. BURGESS, M.A.S., 'The Age of Classicism', in An Introduction to Russian Language and Literature (Cambridge, 1977), 111-32 (Companion to Russian Studies, 2), edited by R. AUTY and D. OBOLENSKY.

90. The Modern Encyclopedia of Russian and Soviet Literature, edited by H.B. WEBER (Gulf Breeze, 1977-).

91. CRONIN, V., Catherine Empress of All the Russias (1978).
(Pp. 222-34, 'The Literary Scene'; pp. 235-45, 'Of Palaces and Paintings').

92. DRAGE, C.L., Russian Literature in the Eighteenth Century. The Solemn Ode. The Epic. Other Poetic Genres. The Story. The Novel. Drama. An Introduction for University Courses (1978).

93. LIKHACHEV, D.S., 'The Petrine Reforms and the Development of Russian Culture', CSS, XIII, 1/2(1979), 230-34.

94. BROWN, W.E., A History of 18th Century Russian Literature (Ann Arbor, 1980).

95. MADARIAGA, I.DE, Russia in the Age of Catherine the Great (1981).
(Chapter 22, 'Court and Culture'; Chapter 33, 'The Role of Freemasonry'; Chapter 34, 'The Birth of the Intelligentsia').

D. LITERARY MOVEMENTS

96. BUCSELA, J., 'The Problems of Baroque in Russian Literature', RR, XXXI, 3(1973), 260-71.

97. SEGEL, H.B., 'Baroque and Rococo in Eighteenth-Century Russian Literature', CSP, XV, 4(1973), 556-65.

98. SEGEL, H.B., 'Classicism and Classical Antiquity in Eighteenth- and Early Nineteenth-Century Russian Literature', in Garrard, 48-71.

99. NEUHAUSER, R., 'Periodization and Classification of Sentimental and Preromantic Trends in Russian Literature between 1750 and 1815', in Canadian Contributions to the Seventh International Congress of Slavists (The Hague, 1974), 11-39.

100. NEUHAUSER, R., Towards the Romantic Age. Essays on Sentimental and Preromantic Literature in Russia (The Hague, 1974).

101. BAEHR, S.L., 'The Masonic Component in Eighteenth-Century Russian Literature', in Cross, 121-40.

102. JONES, W.G., 'A Trojan Horse Within the Walls of Classicism: Russian Classicism and the National Specific', in Cross, 95-120.

103. SMITH, G.S., 'Sentimentalism and Pre-Romanticism as Terms and Concepts', in Cross, 173-84.

104. FORSYTH, J., 'The "isms" of Eighteenth-Century Russian Literature', British Journal for Eighteenth-Century Studies, I, 3(1978), 193-205.
(A review of Cross).

105. GUKOVSKII, G., 'From "On Russian Classicism"', translated by P.O'MEARA, RLT, 20/21.

106. SERMAN, I.Z., 'The Literary Content in Russian Eighteenth-Century Aesthetics', translated by G.S.SMITH, RLT, 20/21.

E. HISTORY OF IDEAS

107. LANG, D.M., 'Some Forerunners of the Decembrists', Cambridge Journal, I, 10(1948), 623-34.

108. TOMPKINS, S.R., The Russian Mind: From Peter the Great through the Enlightenment (Norman, 1953).

109. ZENKOVSKY, S., A History of Russian Philosophy, I (1953). (Pp. 70-99).

110. ROGGER, H., 'The Russian National Character: Some Eighteenth-Century Views', HSS, IV(1957), 17-34.

111. ROGGER, H., National Consciousness in Eighteenth-Century Russia (Cambridge, Mass., 1960).

112. UTECHIN, S.V., Russian Political Thought: A Concise History (1963). (Pp. 37-70, 'Petrine Russia', deals with the eighteenth century from Prokopovich to Radishchev).

113. A History of Russian Economic Thought: Ninth through Eighteenth Centuries, edited and translated by J.M. LETICHE (Berkeley and Los Angeles, 1964) (Pp. 229-636).

114. McCONNELL, A., 'The Origins of the Russian Intelligentsia', SEEJ, VIII(1964), 1-16.

115. RAEFF, M., The Origins of the Russian Intelligentsia: The Eighteenth-Century Nobility (New York, 1966).

116. RAEFF, M., 'Filling the Gap between Radishchev and the Decembrists', SR, XXVI, 3(1967), 395-413.

117. RYU, IN-HO L., 'Freemasonry under Catherine the Great: A Reinterpretation' (Ph.D., Harvard University, 1967).

118. TUMINS, V.A., 'Enlightenment and Mysticism in Eighteenth-Century Russia', Studies on Voltaire and the Eighteenth Century, LVIII(1967), 1671-88.

119. BOSS, V.J., (Review Essay on) Epokha prosveshcheniia, edited by M.P. ALEKSEEV (Leningrad, 1967), Kritika, V, 1(1968), 25-38.

120. CALINGER, R.S., 'The Introduction of the Newtonian Natural Philosophy into Russia and Prussia (1725-1772)' (Ph.D., University of Chicago, 1971).

121. MERGUERIAN, B.J., 'Political Ideas in Russia during the Period of Peter the Great' (Ph.D., Harvard University, 1971).

122. CLENDENNING, P.H., 'Eighteenth-Century Russian Translators of Western Economic Works', Journal of European Economic History, I, 3(1972), 745-53.

123. OKENFUSS, M., (Review Essay on) A.A. GALAKTIONOV and P.F. NIKANDROV, Russkaia filosofiia XI-XIX vekov (Leningrad, 1970); I.Ia. SHCHIPANOV, Filosofiia russkogo prosveshcheniia (Moscow, 1971); N.F. UTKINA, Estestvennonauchnyi materializm v Rossii XVIII veka (Moscow, 1971), Kritika, XI, 1(1972), 13-32.

124. RAEFF, M., 'The Enlightenment in Russia and Russian Thought in the Enlightenment', in Garrard, 25-47.

125. RYU, IN-HO L., 'Moscow Freemasons and the Rosicrucian Order. A Study in Organisation and Control', in Garrard, 198-232.

126. TREADGOLD, D.W., The West in Russia and China: Religion and Secular Thought in Modern Times, I (Cambridge, 1973). (Pp. 84-136).

127. BENSON, S., 'The Role of Western Political Thought in Petrine Russia', CSS, VIII, 2(1974), 254-74.

128. GLEASON, W., 'Political Ideals and Loyalties of Some Russian Writers of the Early 1760s', SR, XXXIV, 3(1975), 560-75.

129. JAMES, W.A., 'Paul I and the Jesuits in Russia' (Ph.D., University of Washington, 1977).

130. BAEHR, S.L., 'From History to National Myth: Translatio imperii in Eighteenth-Century Russia', RR, XXXVII, 1(1978), 1-13.

131. GLEASON, W., 'Pufendorf and Wolff in the Literature of Catherinian Russia', Germano-Slavica, II, 6(1978), 427-37.

132. TSCHIŽEWSKIJ, D., Russian Intellectual History, translated by J.C. OSBORNE, edited by M.P. RICE (Ann Arbor, 1978). (Pp. 135-82: 'Russia between East and West, 1700-1905').

133. DUKES, P., 'Some Aberdonian Influences on the Early Russian Enlightenment', CSS, XIII, 4(1979), 436-51.

134. PETSCHAUER, P., 'The Philosopher and the Reformer: Tsar Peter I, G.W. Leibnitz and the College System', CSS, XIII, 4 (1979), 473-87.

135. VENTURI, F., 'From Scotland to Russia: An Eighteenth-Century Debate on Feudalism', in GBR, 2-24.

136. WALICKI, A., A History of Russian Thought from the Enlightenment to Marxism, translated by H. ANDREWS-RUSIECKA (Stanford, 1979).

137. BARTLETT, R.P., 'I.E. and the Free Economic Society's Essay
      Competition', _SGECRN_, 8(1980), 58-67.

138. LEONARD, G.I., 'Novikov, Shcherbatov, Radishchev: The
      Intellectual in the Age of Catherine the Great' (Ph.D.,
      State University of New York at Binghampton, 1980).

139. SHATZ, M.S., _Soviet Dissent in Historical Perspective_
      (Cambridge, 1980).
      (Pp. 12-31, 'The Genesis of the Russian Intelligentsia').

140. DUKES, P., 'The Russian Enlightenment', in _The Enlightenment
      in National Context_, edited by R. PORTER and M.TEICH
      (Cambridge, 1981), 176-91.

141. GLEASON, W.J., _Moral Idealists, Bureaucracy, and Catherine
      the Great_ (New Brunswick, N.J., 1981).
      (The ideas of D. and P. Fonvizin, S.G. Domashnev, A.G. Karin,
      I.F. Bogdanovich, N.I. Novikov).

142. ROSENBERG, K., 'The Norman Theory and the Language Question
      in Mid-Eighteenth-Century Russia', _SGECRN_, 10(1982),

143. BAEHR, S.L., 'In the Image and Likeness: the "Political Icon"
      in Seventeenth- and Eighteenth-Century Russia', _RLT_, 20/21.

F. CENSORSHIP, THE PRESS

144. ANON., 'Account of the Political Journals, &c., in Russia', Monthly Magazine, IX(1800), 433-5.

145. SEIDL, G., 'History of Russian Journalism, 18th Century' (Ph.D., University of California, Berkeley, 1956).

146. BAYLEY, R.B., 'Freedom and Regulation of the Russian Periodical Press' (Ph.D., University of Illinois, 1968).

147. PAPMEHL, K.A., Freedom of Expression in Eighteenth Century Russia (The Hague, 1971).

148. CROSS, A.G., 'Printing at Nikolaev, 1798-1803', Transactions of the Cambridge Bibliographical Society, VI, 3(1974), 149-57.

149. LUCAS, R., (Review of) S.P. LUPPOV, Kniga v Rossii v pervoi chetverti XVIII veka, SGECRN, 2(1974), 67-79.

150. MALCOLM, N., 'The Birth of Russian Journalism', Journal of Russian Studies, 31(1976), 17-27.

151. BROWN, J.H., 'The Publication and Distribution of the Trudy of the Free Economic Society, 1765-1796', RR, XXXVI(1977), 341-50.

152. MARKER, G.J., 'Publishing and the Formation of a Reading Public in Eighteenth-Century Russia' (Ph.D., University of California, Berkeley, 1977).

153. MARKER, G.J., 'Russia and the "Printing Revolution": Notes and Observations', SR, 41, 2(1982), 266-83.

G. CONTACTS WITH FOREIGN

LITERATURE AND CULTURE

i. General

154. LINCOLN, W.B., 'Western Culture Comes to Russia', HT, XX, 10 (1970), 677-85.

155. BERMAN, M.H. (HEIM, M.H.), 'Trediakovskij, Sumarokov and Lomonosov as Translators of West European Literature' (Ph.D., Harvard University, 1971).

156. HEIM, M.H., 'Two Approaches to Translation: Sumarokov vs. Trediakovskij', in Mnemozina. Studia litteraria russica in honorem Vsevolod Setchkarev, edited by J.T. BAUER and N.W. INGHAM (Munich, 1974), 185-92.

157. WILBERGER, C.H., 'Comrade Philosophe: Russia and the West in the Eighteenth Century', Proceedings of the Pacific Northwest Conference on Foreign Languages, XXVI(1975), 65-8.

158. ANDERSON, M.S., Peter the Great (1978).
(Pp. 113-25, 'Intellectual and Cultural Life').

159. CROSS, A.G, The 1780s: Russia under Western Eyes. Catalogue of an Exhibition (Norwich, 1981).

ii. Britain

160. MATTHEWS, W.K., 'English Influence in Russian Literature 1700-1830' (M.A., University of Manchester, 1923).

161. MANNING, C.A., 'Russian Translation of Paradise Lost', SEER, XIII(1934), 173-6.

162. SIMMONS, E.J., English Literature and Culture in Russia (1553-1840) (Cambridge, Mass., 1935).

163. ALEKSEEV, M.P., 'Adam Smith and his Russian Admirers', in Adam Smith as Student and Professor, edited by W.R. SCOTT (Glasgow, 1937), 424-31.

164. GIBIAN, G.J., 'Shakespeare in Russia' (Ph.D., Harvard University, 1951).

165. ALEKSEEV, M.P., 'Fielding in the Russian Language', VOKS Bulletin, LXXXVII, 4(1954), 88-92.

166. BREWSTER, D., East-West Passage (1954).
(Pp. 20-33).

167. MALNICK, B., 'David Garrick and the Russian Theatre', _MLR_, L, 1(1955), 173-5.

168. ANDERSON, M.S., _Britain's Discovery of Russia 1553-1815_ (1958).

169. BERKOV, P.N., 'English Plays in St Petersburg in the 1760's and 1770's', _OSP_, VIII(1958), 90-97.

170. ANDERSON, M.S., 'Some British Influences on Russian Intellectual Life and Society in the Eighteenth Century', _SEER_, XXXIX(1960), 148-63.

171. BIDA, C., 'Shakespeare in Polish and Russian Classicism and Romanticism', _Études slaves et est-européennes_, VI(1961),188-95.

172. HEIER, E., 'William Robertson and Ludwig Heinrich von Nicolay, His German Translator at the Court of Catherine II', _Scottish Historical Review_, XLI, 132(1962), 135-40.

173. SIMMONS, J.S.G., 'Samuel Johnson "On the Banks of the Wolga"', _OSP_, XI(1964), 28-37.

174. SIMMONS, J.S.G., 'Samuel Johnson "On the Banks of the Neva": A Note on a Picture by Reynolds in the Hermitage', in _Johnson, Boswell, and their Circle: Essays Presented to L.F. Powell_ (Oxford, 1965), 208-14.

175. CRAVEN, K., 'Laurence Sterne and Russia: Four Case Studies' (Ph.D., Columbia University, 1967).

176. PITCHER, H., 'A Scottish View pf Catherine's Russia: William Richardson's _Anecdotes of the Russian Empire_ (1784)', _Forum for Modern Language Studies_, III, 3(1967), 236-51.

177. SMITH, I.H., 'An English View of Russia in the Early Eighteenth Century', _CSS_, I, 2(1967), 276-83. (On Daniel Defoe).

178. PAPMEHL, K.A., 'Samuel Bentham and the _Sobesednik_, 1783', _SEER_, XLVI(1968), 210-19.

179. CROSS, A.G., 'Arcticus and _The Bee_', _OSP_, NS II(1969), 62-76. (On Matthew Guthrie).

180. CROSS, A.G., 'The Reverend William Tooke's Contribution to English Knowledge of Russia at the End of the Eighteenth Century', _CSS_, III, 1(1969), 106-15.

181. PAPMEHL, K.A., 'Matthew Guthrie--The Forgotten Student of Eighteenth-Century Russia', _CSP_, XI, 2(1969), 167-81.

182. ARINSHTEIN, L.M., 'Pope in Russian Translations of the Eighteenth Century', _Studies in Bibliography: Papers of the Bibliographical Society of the University of Virginia_, XXIV (1971), 166-75.

183. MARTYNOV, I.F., 'English Literature and Eighteenth-Century Russian Reviewers', OSP, NS IV(1971), 30-42.

184. BOSS, V., Newton and Russia: The Early Influence, 1698-1796 (Cambridge, Mass., 1972).

185. BARRATT, G.R., 'The Melancholy and the Wild: A Note on Macpherson's Russian Success', Studies in Eighteenth-Century Culture, III(1973), 125-35.

186. CROSS, A.G., 'The British in Catherine's Russia', in Garrard, 233-63.

187. DUKES, P., 'Ossian and Russia', Scottish Literary News, III, 3(1973), 17-21.

188. BROWN, A.H., 'S.E.Desnitsky, Adam Smith and the Nakaz of Catherine II', OSP, NS VII(1974), 42-59.

189. CROSS, A.G., 'The English Garden and Russia: An Anonymous Identified', SGECRN, 2(1974), 25-9. (George Mason, 1768)

190. BARRATT, G.R., 'James Thomson in Russia: The Changing of The Seasons', Comparative Literature Studies, XII, 4(1975), 367-73.

191. CROSS, A.G., 'Russian Students in Eighteenth-Century Oxford (1766-1775)', Journal of European Studies, V(1975), 91-110.

192. CROSS, A.G., 'Yakov Smirnov: A Russian Priest of Many Parts', OSP, NS VIII(1975), 37-52.

193. PUSHCHIN, H.A., 'German and English Influences on the Russian Romantic Literary Ballad' (Ph.D., New York University, 1976).

194. CROSS, A.G., 'A Letter of 1747 from the Norfolk Record Office', SGECRN, 5(1977), 66-9.
(From P.Kostiurin to Rev. Johns of Limpsfield, 1747).

195. CROSS, A.G., Anglo-Russian Relations in the Eighteenth Century: Catalogue of an Exhibition (Norwich, 1977).

196. CROSS, A.G., 'A Russian Engineer in Eighteenth-Century Britain: The Diary of N.I. Korsakov, 1776-7', SEER, LV(1977), 1-20.

197. CROSS, A.G., 'Some Anglo-Russian Poetic Curiosities of the Eighteenth Century', SGECRN, 5(1977), 15-26.
(Moses Stringer, Mrs Mary Pix, Aaron Hill, James Thomson, Rev. Peter Cunningham, Robert Merry, W. Nisbet, "Musaphilus" (William Richardson?), Lord Frederick North).

198. SMITH, G.S., 'An Unknown Translated Panegyric Poem of 1737: Michael Maittaire and Prince Antiokh Kantemir', SEER, LV (1977), 161-71.

199. CROSS, A.G., 'Notes to an Exhibition of Eighteenth-Century Books of Anglo-Russian Interest from the Morfill Collection in the Taylor Institution Library, University of Oxford, Mounted for the 20th Meeting of the Study Group', <u>SGECRN</u>, 6(1978), 17-25.

200. SMITH, C.N., 'French's 'Ode to Suwarrow'', <u>SGECRN</u>, 6(1978), 54-7.

201. BRIDGES, R.M., 'A Possible Source for Daniel Defoe's <u>The Farther Adventures of Robinson Crusoe</u>', <u>British Journal for Eighteenth-Century Studies</u>, II, 3(1979), 231-6.
(Adam Brand, <u>A Journal of the Embassy from their Majesties John and Peter Alexievitz...</u> (London, 1698)).
(See No. 208 below).

202. CROSS, A.G., '"By the Banks of the Thames": Russians in Eighteenth-Century Britain', in <u>GBR</u>, 25-46.

203. <u>Great Britain and Russia in the Eighteenth Century: Contacts and Comparisons</u>, edited by A.G. CROSS (Newtonville, 1979).

204. HOME, R.W., 'Scientific Links between Britain and Russia in the Second Half of the Eighteenth Century', in <u>GBR</u>, 212-24.

205. LEVIN, Iu.D., 'Russian Responses to the Poetry of Ossian', in <u>GBR</u>, 46-64.

206. RAUCH, G. VON, 'Political Preconditions for East-West Cultural Relations in the Eighteenth Century', <u>CSS</u>, XIII, 4(1979), 391-411.

207. CROSS, A.G., <u>"By the Banks of the Thames": Russians in Eighteenth-Century Britain</u> (Newtonville, 1980).

208. CROSS, A.G., 'Don't Shoot Your Russianists: Or, Defoe and Adam Brand', <u>British Journal for Eighteenth-Century Studies</u>, III, 3(1980), 230-33.
(A reply to Bridges, No.201).

209. PAPMEHL, K.A., 'An Eighteenth-Century English Translation of a Ukrainian Folk-Song', <u>CSP</u>, XXIV(1982), 175-80.
(Matthew Guthrie's translation from the Prach collection).

iii. France

210. MOHRENSCHILDT, D. VON, <u>Russia in the Life of Eighteenth-Century France</u> (New York, 1936).

211. OUSTINOFF, P.C., 'Notes on Diderot's Fortunes in Russia', _Diderot Studies_, I(1949), 121-42.

212. KARLINSKY, S., 'Tallemant and the Beginning of the Novel in Russia', _Comparative Literature_, XV, 3(1963), 226-33.

213. McCONNELL, A., 'Helvétius' Russian Pupils', _The Journal of the History of Ideas_, XXIV, 3(1963), 373-86.

214. TUMINS, V.A., 'Voltaire and the Rise of Russian Drama', _Studies on Voltaire and the Eighteenth Century_, XXVII1963), 1689-1701.

215. LENTIN, A., 'Voltaire and Peter the Great', _HT_, XVIII, 10 (1968), 683-9.

216. DAY, H.R., 'Voltaire's Portrayal of Peter the Great' (Ph.D., Boston University, 1971).

217. LENTIN, A., 'Introduction', in V.A. BIL'BASOV, _Didro v Peterburge_ (Reprint, Cambridge, 1972), 1-27.

218. LOJKINE, A.K., 'Molière in Russia in the XVIII Century', _AUMLA_, 39(1973), 85-93.

219. WILSON, A., 'Diderot in Russia, 1773-1774', in _Garrard_, 166-97.

220. WILBERGER, C.H., 'A Tale of Four Travellers: American and Russian Views of Eighteenth-Century France', _Proceedings of the Pacific Northwest Conference of Modern Languages_, XXVIII, 2(1977), 39-42.

221. MILLER, A., 'Rousseau's _Confessions_ in Russian Criticism: The Pre-Soviet Period', _Oeuvres et Critiques_, III, 1(1978), 115-23.

iv. Germany

222. COLEMAN, A.P., 'Kotzebue and Russia', _Germanic Review_, V, 4 (1930), 323-44.

223. COLEMAN, A.P., 'The Siberian Exile of Kotzebue', _Germanic Review_, VI, 3(1931), 244-55.

224. KEEFER, L., 'Herder's Russian Utopia', _Modern Language Notes_, LI(1936), 551-9.

225. BISSONNETTE, G.L., 'Pufendorf and the Church Reforms of Peter the Great' (Ph.D., Columbia University, 1962).

226. DAVID, Z.V., 'The Influence of Jacob Boehme on Russian Religious Thought', SR, XXI, 1(1962), 43-64.

227. GRONICKA, A.VON, 'Early Russian Reaction to Goethe and his Work', Germanic Review, XXXVII, 2(1963), 137-50.

228. GESEMANN, W., 'Herder's Russia', Journal of the History of Ideas, XXVI, 3(1965), 424-34.

229. GRONICKA, A.VON, The Russian Image of Goethe: Goethe in Russian Literature of the First Half of the Nineteenth Century (Philadelphia, 1968).
(Pp. 7-31).

230. MARCELL, N., 'The Impact and Influence of Russian Literature upon German Writers in the Eighteenth and the Beginning of the Nineteenth Centuries' (Ph.D., University of Illinois, 1970).

231. McGOLDRICK, J.J., 'Russia in the Writings of August von Kotzebue: A Study of his Satire and Irony' (Ph.D., State University of New York at Buffalo, 1975).

v. United States of America

232. DVOICHENKO-MARKOVA, E., 'Benjamin Franklin, the American Philosophical Society, and the Russian Academy of Science', Proceedings of the American Philosophical Society, XCI(1947), 25-57.

233. DVOICHENKO-MARKOVA, E., 'The American Philosophical Society and Early Russian-American Relations', Proceedings of the American Philosophical Society, XCIV(1950), 549-610.

234. LASERSON, M.M., The American Impact on Russia 1784-1917 (New York, 1950).

235. OHLOBLYN, A., 'The American Revolution and Ukrainian Liberation Ideas during the late 18th Century', Ukrainian Quarterly, XI(1955), 203-12.

236. SHPRYGOVA, M.R., 'The American War of Independence as Treated by N.I. Novikov's Moscow Gazette', Studies in Soviet History, I(1962), 51-62.

237. BOLKHOVITINOV, N.N., 'Beginnings of the Establishment of Scientific and Cultural Relations between America and Russia', Soviet Review, VII, 4(1966-7), 3-14.

238. The American Image of Russia, 1775-1917, edited by E.ANSCHEL (New York, 1974).

239. BOLKHOVITINOV, N.N., The Beginnings of Russian-American Relations, 1775-1815 (Cambridge, Mass., 1975).

240. BOLKHOVITINOV, N.N., Russia and the American Revolution (Tallahassee, 1976).

vi. Others

241. TURKEVICH, L.B., Cervantes in Russia (Princeton, 1950).

242. CIZOVA, T., 'Beccaria in Russia', SEER, XL(1962), 384-408.

243. SCHANZER, G.O., '"Lazarillo de Tormes" in Eighteenth-Century Russia', in Symposium of St John's University (New York, 1962), 54-62.

244. WELSH, D.J., 'Metastasio's Reception in 18th Century Poland and Russia', Italica, XLI, 1(1964), 41-6.

245. BATALDEN, S.K., 'Eugenios Voulgaris in Russia, 1771-1806: A Chapter in Greco-Slavic Ties of the Eighteenth Century' (Ph.D., University of Minnesota, 1975).

246. SAUNDERS, D.B., 'The Political and Cultural Impact of the Ukraine on Great Russia, c. 1775-c. 1835' (D.Phil., Oxford University, 1979).

247. LEWIN, P., 'Polish-Ukrainian-Russian Literary Relations of the Sixteenth-Eighteenth Centuries: New Approaches', SEEJ, XXIV, 3(1980), 256-69.

248. SMITH, C.N., 'Ferdinand Kauer and the Siege of Ochakov', SGECRN, 8(1980), 46-51.
(The Austrian composer (1751-1831) and his Sonata Militaire).

H. TRAVELLERS TO,
AND FOREIGN RESIDENTS IN,
RUSSIA

249. BABEY, A.M., _Americans in Russia 1776-1917: A Study of the American Travelers in Russia from the American Revolution to the Russian Revolution_ (New York, 1938).

250. DVOICHENKO-MARKOVA, E., 'John Ledyard and the Russians', _RR_, XI(1952), 211-22.

251. PUTNAM, P., _Seven Britons in Imperial Russia (1689-1812)_ (Princeton, 1952).

252. ANDERSON, M.S., 'Samuel Bentham in Russia, 1779-1791', _SR_ XV, 2(1956), 157-72.

253. HANS, N., 'François Pierre Pictet: Secretary to Catherine II', _SEER_, XXXVI(1958), 481-91.

254. KIRCHNER, W., 'Samuel Bentham and Siberia', _SEER_, XXXVI(1958), 471-80.

255. BISCHOFF, I., 'Madame Vigée Le Brun at the Court of Catherine the Great', _RR_, XXIV(1965), 30-45.

256. BISCHOFF, I., 'Étienne Maurice Falconet: Sculptor of the Statue of Peter the Great', _RR_, XXIV(1965), 369-86.

257. IGNATIEFF, L., 'French Émigrés in Russia after the French Revolution', _CSP_, VIII(1966), 125-31.

258. PAPMEHL, K.A., 'The Regimental Schools Established in Siberia by Samuel Bentham', _CSP_, VIII(1966), 153-68.

259. CHRISTIE, I.R., 'Samuel Bentham and the Western Colony at Krichev, 1784-1787', _SEER_, XLVIII(1970), 232-47.

260. WILSON, F., _Russia through Foreign Eyes, 1553-1900_ (1970).

261. CROSS, A.G., 'An Oxford Don in Catherine the Great's Russia', _Journal of European Studies_, I, 2(1971), 166-74.

262. CROSS, A.G., 'British Freemasons in Russia during the Reign of Catherine the Great', _OSP_, NS IV(1971), 43-72.

263. CROSS, A.G., _Russia under Western Eyes, 1517-1825_ (1971).

264. CROSS, A.G., 'Chaplains to the British Factory in St Petersburg, 1723-1813', _European Studies Review_, II, 2(1972), 125-42.

265. HOME, R.W., 'Science as a Career in Eighteenth-Century Russia: The Case of F.U.T. Aepinus', <u>SEER</u>, LI(1973), 75-94.

266. BARTLETT, R.P., 'Foreign Settlement in Russia under Catherine II', <u>New Zealand Slavonic Journal</u>, NS 1(1974), 1-22.

267. CROSS, A.G., 'James Walker's <u>Paramythia</u>', <u>SGECRN</u>, 3(1975), 41-51.

268. HOME, R.W., 'Introduction', in <u>Aepinus's Essay on the Theory of Electricity and Magnetism.</u> Introductory Monograph and Notes by R.W. HOME. Translation by P.J. CONNOR (Princeton, 1979), 3-226.

I. POETRY

269. [LEEDS, W.H.],'Russian Fabulists, with Specimens', _Fraser's Magazine_, XIX(1839), 153-63.
   (Discusses A.P. Sumarokov, p.156).

270. [LEEDS, W.H.],'Russian Fabulists, with Specimens', _Fraser's Magazine_, XXV(1842), 237-50.
   (Discusses Pankratii Sumarokov, pp. 240-42).

271. NEWMARCH, R., _Poetry and Progress in Russia_ (1907).
   (Pp. 6-23, 'The Precursors of Pushkin').

272. BURGI, R., _A History of the Russian Hexameter_ (Hamden, 1954).

273. HOULDSWORTH, H.F., 'A Comparative Study of the Fable in France, Germany and Russia, with Special Reference to Krylov and La Fontaine' (M.A., University of Nottingham, 1955).

274. UNBEGAUN, B.O., _Russian Versification_ (Oxford, 1956; revised edition, Oxford, 1963).

275. DRAGE, C.L., 'Trochaic Metres in Russian Syllabo-Tonic Poetry from Trediakovsky to Krylov' (M.A., University of London, 1959).

276. SEAMAN, G.R., 'Russian Folk-Song in the Eighteenth Century', _Music and Letters_, XL, 3(1959), 253-60.

277. DRAGE, C.L., 'Trochaic Metres in Early Russian Syllabo-Tonic Poetry', _SEER_, XXXVIII(1960), 361-79.

278. DRAGE, C.L., 'The Rhythmic Development of the Trochaic Tetrameter in Early Russian Syllabo-Tonic Poetry', _SEER_, XXXIX(1961), 346-68.

279. DRAGE, C.L., 'The _Anacreontea_ and 18th-Century Russian Poetry', _SEER_, XLI(1962), 110-34.

280. VICKERY, W.N., '"Mednyj vsadnik" and the Eighteenth-Century Heroic Ode', _Indiana Slavic Studies_, III(1963), 140-62.

281. NABOKOV, V., 'The Origination of Metrical Verse in Russia', in _Eugene Onegin. A Novel in Verse by Aleksandr Pushkin. Translated from the Russian, with a Commentary, by Vladimir Nabokov_, III(1964), 478-91.

282. BUCSELA, J., 'The Birth of Russian Syllabo-Tonic Versification', _SEEJ_, IX(1965), 281-94.

283. MARKOV, V., 'Russian Poetry', in _Encyclopedia of Poetry and Poetics_, edited by A. PREMINGER (Princeton, 1965), 727-36.
   (Pp. 728-9).

284. SILBAJORIS, R., _Russian Versification. The Theories of Trediakovskii, Lomonosov, and Kantemir_ (New York, 1968).

285. SULLIVAN, J., and DRAGE, C.L., 'Poems in an Unpublished Manuscript of the _Vinograd rossiiskii_', _OSP_, NS I(1968), 27-48.

286. HAMMOND, K.G., 'The Metrical and Rhythmical Development of the Russian Fable in the Eighteenth Century' (Ph.D., University of London, 1970).

287. JENSEN, K.B., and MØLLER, P.U., 'Paraphrase and Style: A Stylistic Analysis of Trediakovskij's, Lomonosov's and Sumarokov's Paraphrases of the 143rd Psalm', _Scando-Slavica_, XVI(1970), 57-73.

288. McMILLIN, A.B., and DRAGE, C.L., '_Kuranty_: An Unpublished Russian Songbook of 1733', _OSP_, NS III(1970), 1-31.

289. DABARS, Z.D., 'The Simile in the Poetry of Sumarokov, Karamzin, and Deržavin' (Ph.D., Indiana University, 1971).

290. BAEHR, S.L., 'The Utopian Mode in Eighteenth-Century Russian Panegyric Poetry' (Ph.D., Columbia University, 1972).

291. WORTH, D.S., 'On Eighteenth-Century Russian Rhyme', _Russian Literature_, 3(1972), 47-74.

292. COOPER, B.F., 'The History and Development of the Ode in Russia' (Ph.D., Cambridge University, 1973).

293. CROUCHER, M., 'The Relation of Genre to the Incidence of the Dactylic Caesura in the Russian Six-Foot Iamb during the Eighteenth Century' (M.A., University of North Carolina, Chapel Hill, 1973).

294. GARRISON, W.S., 'A Preliminary Study in the Problem of Genre in Relation to the Incidence of the Dactylic Caesura in the Russian Six-Foot Iamb: M.V. Lomonosov and A.P. Sumarokov' (M.A., University of North Carolina, Chapel Hill, 1973).

295. SMITH, G.S., 'The Contribution of Glück and Paus to the Development of Russian Versification: The Evidence of Rhyme and Stanza Forms', _SEER_, LI(1973), 22-35.

296. VICKERY, W.N., 'On the Question of the Emergence of the Dactylic Caesura in the Russian Eighteenth-Century Six-Foot Iamb', _International Journal of Slavic Linguistics and Poetics_, XVI(1973), 147-56.

297. DABARS, Z.D., 'The Simile in the Poetry of Sumarokov, Karamzin and Derzhavin', _Russian Literature Triquarterly_, 7(1974), 387-406.

298. EEKMAN, T., _The Realm of Rhyme_ (Amsterdam, 1974).
(Pp. 97-116).

299. BARRATT, G.R., 'Poetry as Paysage (1780-1830): A Note on
Russian _Berglust_', MSlS, 9/10(1975), 140-47.

300. SMITH, G.S., 'A.V. Pozdneev and the Russian 'Literary Song',
Journal of European Studies, V(1975), 177-89.

301. DRAGE, C.L., 'The Introduction of Russian Syllabo-Tonic
Prosody', SEER, LIV(1976), 481-503.

302. HART, P.R., 'Continuity and Change in the Russian Ode', in
Cross, 45-66.

303. KATZ, M.R., _The Literary Ballad in Early Nineteenth-Century
Russian Literature_ (Oxford, 1976).
(Pp. 3-36).

304. RICE, J.L., 'A Russian Bawdy Song of the Eighteenth Century',
SEEJ, XX(1976), 533-70.

305. LEVITSKY, A., 'The Sacred Ode in Eighteenth-Century Russian
Literary Culture' (Ph.D., University of Michigan, 1977).

306. SMITH, G.S., 'The Reform of Russian Versification: What More
is there to Say?', SGECRN, 5(1977), 39-44.

307. SMITH, G.S., 'The Stanza Forms of Russian Poetry from
Polotsky to Derzhavin' (Ph.D., University of London, 1977).

308. ZELENAK, J., 'The Epigraph in Russian Poetry: Its
Chronological Development from its Origins to the End of the
Nineteenth Century' (Ph.D., University of California, Los
Angeles, 1977).

309. SULLIVAN, J., and DRAGE, C.L., _An Unpublished Religious
Song-Book of Mid-Eighteenth-Century Russia_ (1978).
(Pp. 1-10, 'Eighteenth-Century Manuscript Song-Books').

310. KOCHIS, B.E., 'Literary Equivalence in the Russian Eighteenth
Century Anacreontic' (Ph.D., University of Michigan, 1979).

311. LILLY, I.K., 'On Adjacent and Nonadjacent Russian Rhyme
Pairs', SEEJ, XXIV, 3(1980), 245-55.
(Based on material from Russian poetry, 1740-1800).

312. LILLY, I.K., 'On the Rich Rhymes of M.N. Murav'jev',
International Journal of Slavic Linguistics and Poetics,
XXIII(1981),147-61.

313. BAILEY, J., 'The Versification of the Russian _Kant_ from the
End of the Seventeenth to the Middle of the Eighteenth
Century', _Russian Literature_, XIII(1983), 123-73.

314. SMITH, G.S., 'The Stanza Typology of Russian Poetry
1735-1816: A General Survey', _Russian Literature_, XIII(1983),
175-203.

315. MARKOV, V., 'Three Poets', _RLT_, 20/21.
(P. Buslaev, V.K. Trediakovskii, and M.N. Murav'ev)

J. PROSE

316. MENUT, A.D., 'Russian Courtesy Literature in the 18th Century', _Symposium_, III(1949), 76-90.

317. GOODLIFFE, J.D., 'Some Comments on Narrative Prose Fiction in Eighteenth-Century Russian Literature, with Special Reference to Čulkov', _MSlS_, 5/6(1971), 124-36.

318. WHITE, R.S., 'The Development of Russian Prose in the Early Eighteenth Century' (Ph.D., University of Michigan, 1971).

319. WILSON, R.K., _The Literary Travelogue: A Comparative Study with Special Reference to Russian Literature from Fonvizin to Pushkin_ (The Hague, 1973).

320. PARTHÉ, K., 'All Strange Wonders: Literature of Travel in Russia, 1700-1820' (M.A., Cornell University, 1973).

321. RANSEL, D., 'Bureaucracy and Patronage: The View from an Eighteenth-Century Russian Letter-Writer', in _The Rich and Well Born and the Powerful: Elites and Upper Classes in History_, edited by F.C. JAHER (Urbana-Chicago-London, 1973), 154-78.
(On a letter-writing manual of 1788).

322. GLOWACKI-PRUS, X., 'A Brief Survey of Memoirs Written in Russian from Peter the Great to S.T.Aksakov', _New Zealand Slavonic Journal_, 12(1974), 10-26.

323. NEUENSCHWANDER, D.B., 'Themes in Russian Utopian Fiction: A Study in the Utopian Works of M.M. Shcherbatov, A. Ulybyshev, F.V. Bulgarin, and V.F. Odoevsky' (Ph.D., Syracuse University, 1974).

324. BAYKOV-ARIAN, I., 'The Beginnings of Russian Fiction', in _The Modern World, I. Hopes_, edited by D. DAICHES and A.K. THORLBY (1975), 473-511 (_Literature and Western Civilization_).

325. HOPKINS, W.H., 'The Development of 'Pornographic' Literature in Eighteenth- and Early Nineteenth-Century Russia' (Ph.D., Indiana University, 1977).

326. BUDGEN, D.E., 'The Concept of Fiction in Eighteenth-Century Russian Letters', in _GBR_, 65-74.

327. JONES, W.G., 'The Russian View of Eighteenth-Century English Moral Satire: Palliative or Purgative?', in _GBR_, 75-83.

K. THEATRE

328. ANON., 'The Present Situation of Kotzebue, and of the Russian Stage', The German Museum, or Monthly Repository of the Literature of Germany, the North and the Continent in general, III(1801), 114-16.

329. KREMLOV, A., 'Two Commemorative Festivals', translated by G. SHEPHERD, Anglo-Russian Literary Society Proceedings, 29(1900), 91-6.
(On Fedor Volkov).

330. Russian Drama (London-New York-Philadelphia, 1903). (The Drama; its History, Literature, and Influence on Civilization, edited by A. BATES, XVIII).
(Pp. 1-74).

331. ANON., 'Russian Stage: 1. From its Origins to 1762', Twentieth-Century Russia (April, 1916), 169-79.

332. COLEMAN, A.P., Humor in the Russian Comedy from Catherine to Gogol (New York, 1925).

333. FINDEIZEN, N., 'The Earliest Russian Operas', Musical Quarterly (July, 1933), 331-40.

334. MALNICK, B., 'The Origins and Early History of the Theatre in Russia, 1672-1756' (Ph.D., University of London, 1936).

335. MALNICK, B., 'The Origins and Early History of the Theatre in Russia', SEER, XIX(1940), 203-27.

336. MARSDEN, C., Palmyra of the North: The First Days of St. Petersburg (1942).
(Pp. 161-81).

337. ILYIN, E.K., (On Michael Maddox), World Review (February, 1950), 17-22.

338. LEWITTER, L.R., 'A Study of the Academic Drama in Russia and the Ukraine in the Seventeenth and Eighteenth Centuries, with special reference to its Polish Origins' (Ph.D., Cambridge University, 1950).

339. VARNEKE, B.V., History of the Russian Theatre (New York, 1951).
(Pp. 35-151).

340. MALNICK, B., 'Russian Serf Theatres', SEER, XXX(1952), 393-411.

341. BURGESS, M.A.S., 'A Survey of the Stage in Russia from 1741 to 1783, with special reference to the Development of the Russian Theatre' (Ph.D., Cambridge University, 1953).

342. LIFAR, S., _A History of Russian Ballet from its Origins to the Present Day_. Translated by A. HASKELL (1954). (Pp. 19-43).

343. MALNICK, B., 'The Theory and Practice of Russian Drama in the Early 19th Century', _SEER_, XXXIV(1955), 10-33.

344. PARGMENT, L., 'Serf Theatres and Serf Actors', _AATSEEL Journal_, XIV, 3(1956), 71-8.

345. BURGESS, M.A.S., 'Russian Public Theatre Audiences of the 18th and Early 19th Centuries', _SEER_, XXXVII(1958), 160-83.

346. WHAPLES, M.K., 'Eighteenth-Century Russian Opera in the Light of Soviet Scholarship', _Indiana Slavic Studies_, II(1958), 113-34.

347. BURGESS, M.A.S., 'Fairs and Entertainers in 18th-Century Russia', _SEER_, XXXVIII(1959), 95-113.

348. SEAMAN, G.R., 'The National Element in Early Russian Opera, 1779-1800', _Music and Letters_, XLIV, 3(1961), 252-62.

349. SLONIM, M., _Russian Theatre from the Empire to the Soviets_ (Cleveland, 1961). (Pp. 17-37).

350. SEAMAN, G.R., 'The Influence of Folk-Song on Russian Opera up to the Time of Glinka' (D.Phil., Oxford University, 1962).

351. SEAMAN, G.R., 'Folk-Song in Russian Opera of the 18th Century', _SEER_, XLI(1962), 144-57.

352. SIMMONS, R.W.jr, 'Some Notes on Comparative Drama in the Seventeenth and Eighteenth Centuries: Russian, Polish, and German', _Theatre Research_, II(1964), 13-17.

353. WELSH, D.J., '"Philosophers" and "Alchemists" in Some Eighteenth-Century Russian Comedies', _SEER_, XLII(1964), 149-58.

354. WELSH, D.J., 'Satirical Themes in 18th-Century Russian Comedies', _SEER_, XLII(1964), 403-14.

355. WELSH, D.J., _Russian Comedy 1765-1823_ (The Hague-Paris, 1966).

356. SHATZ, M.S., 'The Noble Landowner in Russian Comic Operas of the Time of Catherine the Great: The Patriarchal Image', _CSS_, III, 1(1969), 22-38.

357. BURGESS, M.A.S., 'The First Russian Actor-Manager and the Rise of Repertory in Russia during the Reign of the Empress Elizabeth Petrovna', in Gorski vijenats: A Garland of Essays Offered to Professor Elizabeth Mary Hill, edited by R. AUTY et alii (Cambridge, 1970), 57-84.

358. FOOKS, J.B., 'The Serf Theater of Imperial Russia' (Ph.D., University of Kansas, 1970).

359. WARNER, E.A., 'The Russian Folk-Theatre' (Ph.D., Edinburgh University, 1970).

360. SEAMAN, G.R., 'Russian Opera before Glinka', in Russia: Essays in History and Literature, edited by L.H. LEGTERS (Leiden, 1972), 56-78.

361. STEELE, E., and WELSH, D.J., 'The Commedia dell'arte in Eighteenth-Century Poland and Russia', Forum Italicum, IX, 4(1975), 409-17.

362. CROSS, A.G., 'Mr Fisher's Company of English Actors in Eighteenth-Century Petersburg', SGECRN, 4(1976), 49-56.

363. GOTT, T., 'Low Elements in the Language of 18th-Century Russian Comedy', MSlS, 11(1976), 80-83.

364. BURGESS, M.A.S., 'The Early Theatre', in An Introduction to Russian Language and Literature (Cambridge, 1977), 231-43. (Companion to Russian Studies, 2), edited by R. AUTY and D. OBOLENSKY.

365. LEWIN, P., 'The Ukrainian Popular Religious Stage of the Seventeenth and Eighteenth Centuries on the Territory of the Polish Commonwealth', HSS, I, 3(1977), 308-29.

366. LOJKINE, A.J., 'A Note on the Place of the Comic Opera of the XVIIIth Century in Russian Literature', in Essays to Honour Nina Christesen, edited by J. ARMSTRONG and R. SLOVEK (Kew, Victoria-Balmain,NSW-West Perth,WA, 1977), 102-7.

367. LEWIN, P., 'Early Ukrainian Theater and Drama', Nationalities Papers, VIII, 2(1980), 219-32.

368. LEWIN, P., 'The Staging of Plays at the Kiev Mohyla Academy in the Seventeenth and Eighteenth Centuries', Harvard Ukrainian Studies, V, 3(1981), 320-34.

369. POMAR, M.G., 'The Roots of the Russian Historical Drama: School Drama and Ceremonial Spectacle', Russian Language Journal, XXXV, 121/2(1981), 113-24.

L. SPECIAL TOPICS

370. FRERE, W.H., Some Links in the Chain of Russian Church History (1918).

371. STRUVE, G., 'Russian Eighteenth-Century Literature through Party-Coloured Spectacles', SR, XV, 1(1957).

372. KLEPIKOV, S.A., 'Russian Bookbinding from the Middle of the 17th to the End of the 19th Centuries', Book Collector, XI (1962), 437-47.

373. VUCINICH, A., Science in Russian Culture: A History to 1860 (1965).

374. WORTH, G.H.-, 'Thoughts on the Turning Point in the History of Literary Russian: The Eighteenth Century', International Journal of Slavic Linguistics and Poetics, XIII(1970), 125-35.

375. DUDA, S.T., 'The Theme of the Caucasus in Russian Literature of the XVIII-XIX Centuries' (Ph.D., Vanderbilt University, 1971).

376. KLEPIKOV, S.A., 'Russian Block Books of the Seventeenth and Eighteenth Centuries', Papers of the Bibliographical Society of America, LXXV(1971), 213-24.

377. BRODY, E.C., 'The Demetrius Legend and its Literary Treatment in the Age of the Baroque' (Rutherford, Madison, 1972).

378. WILBERGER, C.H., 'Eighteenth-Century French Scholarship on Russian Literature', Eighteenth-Century Studies, V(1972), 503-26.

379. WILBERGER, C.H., 'Peter the Great: An Eighteenth-Century Hero of Our Times?', Studies on Voltaire and the Eighteenth Century, XCVI(1972), 9-127.

380. MAGGS, B.W., 'China in the Literature of Eighteenth-Century Russia' (Ph.D., University of Illinois, 1973).

381. BLAMBERG, M.O., 'The Publicists of Peter the Great' (Ph.D., Indiana University, 1974).
(Seventeen contemporaries who submitted letters and essays offering proposals for reform).

382. CHOLDIN, M.T., 'Three Early Russian Bibliographers', Library Quarterly, XLIV(1974), 1-28.
(N.I. Novikov, V.S. Sopikov, V.G. Anastasevich).

383. HOLLINGSWORTH, B., 'The Friendly Literary Society', (New Zealand Slavonic Journal, NS 1(1974), 23-41.

384. MAGGS, B.W., 'Eighteenth-Century Russian Reflections on the Lisbon Earthquake, Voltaire and Optimism', Studies on Voltaire and the Eighteenth Century, CXXXVII(1975), 7-29.

385. CROSS, A.G., 'Introduction', in Cross, 5-15.
(The situation of Russian eighteenth-century studies in 1975).

386. CROSS, A.G., '"Nachricht von einigen russischen Schriftstellern" (1768): A New Document and a Bibliography', SGECRN, 4(1976), 32-43.

387. MAGGS, B.W., 'Firework Art and Literature: The Eighteenth-Century Pyrotechnical Tradition in Russia and Western Europe', SEER, LIV(1976), 24-40.

388. TÉTÉNYI, M., 'The Parallel and Diverging Features of XVIIIth Century Russian and Hungarian Literary Development: On Some of the Problems Connected with the Development of the National Literary Language', Acta Litteraria Academiae Scientiarum Hungaricae, 18(1976), 390-98.

389. WILBERGER, C.H., 'Voltaire's Russia: Window on the West', Studies on Voltaire and the Eighteenth Century, CLXIV(1976), 13-287.

390. BUTLER, W.E., 'Foreign Impressions of Russian Law to 1800: Some Reflections', in Russian Law: Historical and Political Perspectives, edited by W.E. BUTLER (Leyden, 1977),

391. MILNER-GULLAND, R., 'Reflections on R. Lucas' "Innovation in Russian Architecture in Early Modern History: A Stylistic Survey"', SGECRN, 5(1977), 45-8.

392. LUCAS, R., 'A Reply', SGECRN, 5(1977), 48-54.
(To R. Milner-Gulland, No. 391).

393. PRESCOTT, J.A., 'The Russian Free Economic Society: Foundation Years', Agricultural History, 51, 3(1977), 503-12.

394. ROWELL, M., Medicinal Plants in Russia in the Eighteenth and Early Nineteenth Centuries' (Ph.D., University of Kansas, 1977).

395. BAEHR, S.L., '"Fortuna redux": The Iconography of Happiness in Eighteenth-Century Russian Courtly Spectacle', in GBR, .109-22.

396. CROSS, A.G., 'British Knowledge of Russian Culture (1698-1801)', CSS, XIII, 4(1979), 412-35.

397. CROSS, A.G., 'The Subscription Library of the British Factory in St Petersburg', SGECRN, 7(1979), 41-6.

398. GASIOROWSKA, X., The Image of Peter the Great in Russian Fiction (Madison, 1979). (Nineteenth- and twentieth-century fiction in the context of eighteenth-century biographies, memoirs and anecdotes about Peter).

399. KOPELEVICH, Iu.Kh., 'The Creation of the Petersburg Academy of Sciences as a New Type of State Institution', in GBR, 204-11.

400. CARVER, S., 'A Reconsideration of Eighteenth-Century Russia's Contributions to European Science', CSS, XIV, 3(1980), 389-405.

401. GRIFFITHS, D.M., 'The Early Years of the Petersburg Academy of Sciences as Reflected in Recent Soviet Literature', CSS, XIV, 3(1980), 436-45.

402. AVERY, R., 'Foreign Influences in the Nautical Terminology of Russian in the 18th Century', OSP, NS XIV(1981), 72-92.

403. TAYLOR, P., 'Russian Music of the Eighteenth Century', Collet's Melodiya Newsletter, 1(1981), 1-8; 2(1981), 1-21.

404. SEAMAN, G., 'An Eighteenth-Century Russian Pocket-Book', SEER; LX(1982), 262-72. (Karmannaia kniga dlia liubitelei muzyki na 1795 god, St. Petersburg, 1795; I.D.Gerstenberg and music publishing).

405. BLACK, J., 'Russia and the British Press, 1720-1740', British Journal for Eighteenth-Century Studies, V, 1(1982), 85-92.

406. For God and Peter the Great: The Works of Thomas Consett, 1723-1729, edited by J. CRACRAFT (Boulder, 1982). (A Reprint of Consett's The Present State and Regulations of the Church of Russia, 1729).

407. SERMAN, I.Z., 'Grigorii Gukovskii', translated by G.S. SMITH, RLT, 20/21.

M. EDUCATION

408. FLORINSKY, M., 'The Bicentenary of the Russian Academy',
     SEER, IV(1925), 396-9.

409. HANS, N.A., 'The Moscow School of Mathematics and Navigation',
     SEER, XXIX(1951), 532-6.

410. LIPSKI, A., 'The Foundation of the Russian Academy of
     Science', Isis, XLIV(1953), 349-54.

411. BRYNER, C., 'Moscow University, 1755-1955', RR, XIV(1955),
     201-13.

412. LIPSKI, A., 'The Beginnings of General Secondary Education in
     Russia', History of Education Journal, VI, 3(1955), 201-10.

413. HANS, N., 'Russian Students at Leyden in the Eighteenth
     Century', SEER, XXXV(1957), 551-62.

414. HANS, N., 'H. Farquharson, Pioneer of Russian Education',
     Aberdeen University Review, XXXVIII, 120(1959), 26-9.

415. HANS, N.A., 'Polish Schools in Russia, 1772-1831', SEER,
     XXXVIII(1960), 391-414.

416. HANS, N.A., 'Dumaresq, Brown and Some Early Educational
     Projects of Catherine II', SEER, XL(1961), 229-35.

417. BISSONNETTE, G., 'Peter the Great and the Church as an
     Educational Institution', in Essays in Russian and Soviet
     History in Honor of Geroid Tanquary Robinson, edited by
     J.S. CURTISS (Leiden, 1963), 3-19.

418. HANS, N.A., The Russian Tradition in Education (1963).
     (Pp.5-19).

419. ROUCEK, J.S., 'Education within the Czarist Framework',
     Pedagogica Historica, IV(1964), 392-443.
     (Pp. 397-410).

420. BECKER, C.B., 'The Church School in Tsarist Social and
     Educational Policy, from Peter to the Great Reforms' (Ph.D.,
     Harvard University, 1965).

421. ALSTON, P.L., Education and the State in Tsarist Russia
     (Cambridge, 1967).
     (Pp. 3-20).

422. CRACRAFT, J., The Church Reform of Peter the Great (1971).

423. OKENFUSS, M.J., 'Education in Russia in the First Half of the
     Eighteenth Century' (Ph.D., Harvard University, 1971).

424. RAEFF, M., _Imperial Russia 1682-1825. The Coming of Age of Modern Russia_ (New York, 1971).
(Pp. 131-58, 'Education and Intelligentsia').

425. OKENFUSS, M.J., 'Technical Training in Russia under Peter the Great', _History of Education Quarterly_, XIII(1973), 325-45.

426. OKENFUSS, M.J., 'The Jesuit Origins of Petrine Education', in _Garrard_, 106-30.

427. OKENFUSS, M.J., 'Russian Students in Europe in the Age of Peter the Great', in _Garrard_, 131-45.

428. BLACK, J.L., 'The Search for a "Correct" Textbook of National History in 18th Century Russia', _The New Review of East-European History_, XVI, 1(1976), 3-19.

429. EPP, G., 'The Educational Policies of Catherine II of Russia, 1762-1796' (Ph.D., University of Manitoba, 1976).

430. BLACK, J.L., 'Citizenship Training and Moral Regeneration as the Mainstay of Russian Schools', _Studies on Voltaire and the Eighteenth Century_, CLXVII(1977), 427-51.

431. FREEZE, G.L., _The Russian Levites: Parish Clergy in the Eighteenth Century_ (Cambridge, Mass., 1977).
(Pp. 78-106, 'The New World of the Seminary').

432. BLACK, J.L., 'Educating Women in Eighteenth-Century Russia: Myths and Realities', _CSP_, XX, 1(1978), 23-43.

433. NASH, C.S., 'The Education of Women in Russia, 1762-1796' (Ph.D., New York University, 1978).

434. BLACK, J.L., _Citizens for the Fatherland: Education, Educators, and Pedagogical Ideals in Eighteenth Century Russia. With a Translation of 'Book on the Duties of Man and Citizen' (St Petersburg, 1783)_ (Boulder-New York, 1979).

435. MADARIAGA, I.DE, 'The Foundation of the Russian Educational System by Catherine II', _SEER_, LVII(1979), 369-95.

436. OKENFUSS, M.J., 'Education and Empire: School Reform in Enlightened Russia', _Jahrbucher für Geschichte Osteuropas_, XXVII, 1(1979), 41-68.
(On J.de Mirievo).

437. WOLKOWSKI, L., 'Polish Commission for National Education, 1773-1794: Its Significance and Influence on Russian and American Education' (Ph.D., Loyola University, 1979).

438. BARTLETT, R.P., 'Culture and Enlightenment: Julius von Canitz and the Kazan' _Gimnazii_ in the Eighteenth Century', _CSS_, XIV, 3(1980), 339-60.

439. OKENFUSS, M.J., _The Discovery of Childhood: The Evidence of the Slavic Primer_ (Newtonville, 1980).

440. OKENFUSS, M.J., 'Popular Educational Tracts in Enlightenment Russia: A Preliminary Survey', _CSS_, XIV, 3(1980), 307-26.

N. PERSONALIA

ABLESIMOV, A.O. (1742-83)

Mel'nik—koldun, obmanshchik i svat (1779)

441. 'The Miller' (Act I), translated by L. WIENER, in Wiener, I, 370-73.

442. The Miller Who Was a Wizard, Cheat and Matchmaker, translated by L. HUGHES, in RLT, 20/21.

443. HUGHES, L., 'Ablesimov's Mel'nik: A Study in Success', SGECRN, 9(1981), 29-40.

ANONYMOUS WORKS

'Akh! daleche v chistom pole'

444. 'Alas! on that plane, distant meadow towers', in Bowring, II, 258-9.

'Akh! kaby na tsvety ne Morosi'

445. 'If the frost nipp'd the flowrets no more', in Bowring, II, 249-50.

'Akh, kak toshno mne toshnen'ko'

446. 'O how gloomy has been to me', in Bowring, II, 251-3.

'Byk ne zakhotel byt' bykom'

447. 'The Ox did not want to be an Ox', translated by P. DUKES, in Dukes, I, 119.

'Chernobrovyi, chernoglazyi'

448. 'Hazel-eyebrow'd, hazel-eyed', in Bowring, II, 264-6.

'Dvorianin i muzhik'

449. 'The Dvorianin and the Muzhik', translated by P. DUKES, in Dukes, I, 117-19.

Gistoriia o rossiiskom matrose Vasilii Koriotskom i o prekrasnoi korolevne Iraklii florenskoi zemli

450. 'The History of the Russian Seaman Vasilii Koriotskii and the Fair Princess Heraclea of the Florentine Kingdom', translated by W.E. HARKINS, in Segel, I, 120-48.

'Na voskhode krasna solnyshka'

451. 'When the lovely sun is mounting high', in <u>Bowring</u>, II, 256-7.

'Ne golubushka v chistom pole vorkuet'

452. 'O'er the meadow not a turtle speeds or flutters', in <u>Bowring</u>, II, 239-41.

'Osen' blednaia v poliakh'

453. 'Autumn's rotes are on the mead', in <u>Bowring</u>, II, 242-5.

<u>Otryvok puteshestviia v *** I*** T***</u> (1772)

454. 'Fragment from a Journey to --- by I... T...', in <u>Brown</u>, 174. (Incomplete).

455. 'Fragment of a Journey from *** by I*** T***', translated by W.G. JONES, in <u>RLT</u>, 20/21.

'Perestan' stonat' kukushechka'

456. 'Listen yet awhile, thou cuckoo dear', in <u>Bowring</u>, II, 263.

'Pesnia' ('Chto ponizhe bylo goroda Saratova')

457. "Song' ('At Saratoff and Tzaritzine'), in <u>Beresford</u>, 40.

<u>Plach kholopov</u>

458. 'The Slave's Lament', translated by P. DUKES, in <u>Dukes</u>, I, 115-17.

'Pover'kh dubchika'

459. 'On an oak there sate', in <u>Bowring</u>, II, 267-9.

'Ty dusha moia'

460. 'O thou soul of mine', in <u>Bowring</u>, II, 260-2.

'Ty prokhodish' dorogaia'

461. 'Ah, thou hurriest by the convent', in <u>Bowring</u>, II, 270-1.

'Ty, vospoi, vospoi zhavoronochik'

462. 'Sing, O sing again, lovely lark of mine', in <u>Bowring</u>, II, 254-5.

'Vysoko sokol letaet'

463. Prose translation, from Prach's collection of 1790, in ANON., review of M. Guthrie, <u>Dissertations sur les antiquités de Russie</u> (1795), <u>The Monthly Review</u>, NS XVIII(1795), 563.

<u>Zhivopisets</u> (See also No.1267)

464. 'Letters to Falalei', translated by W.E. BROWN, <u>Russian Literature Triquarterly</u>, XIV(1976), 304-13.

465. O.N.E., 'Absence' ('Why wilt thou think that thy heart's distress'), in Bowring, I, 195-6.

466. O.N.E., 'Dirge' ('Not to-day be the young rose sought'), in Bowring, I(2nd ed. only), 202.

467. O.N.E., 'Thou Field of my own, thou field so fair', in Bowring, I, 197-8.

468. O.N.E., 'To Mary' ('Noisy Nightingale! be still'), in Bowring, II, 246-8.

469. O.N.E., 'Upon its little turfy hill, the desert's charm and pride', in Bowring, I, 192-4.

470. O.N.E., 'Upon that brow, so soft, so fair', in Bowring, I (2nd ed. only), 201.

471. O.N.E., 'A Young maid sat upon the streamlet's side', in Bowring, I(2nd ed. only), 199-200.

BARKOV, I.S. (1732-68)

'Oda kulachnomu boitsu'(c.1760)

472. 'Ode to a Fist-Fighter', in Brown, 313-15 (extracts).

473. CROSS, A.G., '"The Notorious Barkov": An Annotated Bibliography', SGECRN, 2(1974), 41-52.

474. TARANOVSKY, K., 'The Rhythmical Structure of the Notorious Russian poem Luka', International Journal of Slavic Linguistics and Poetics, XXV/XXVI(1982), 429-32. (Demonstrates that Luka Mudishchev could not have been written by Barkov).

BARSOV, A.A. (1730-91)

Obstoiatel'naia grammatika

475. The Comprehensive Russian Grammar of A.A. Barsov/ Obstoiatel'naia grammatika A.A. Barsova. Critical Edition by L.W. NEWMAN (Columbus, 1980).

BETSKOI, I.I. (1704?-95)

476. RANSEL, D.L., 'Ivan Betskoi and the Institutionalization of the Enlightenment in Russia', CSS, XIV, 3(1980), 327-38.

BOBROV, S.S. (1763?-1810)

'Chertog tvoi vizhdu'

477. 'The Golden Palace', in Bowring, I, 165.

'Izhe Kheruvimy'

478. 'Izhe Kheruvimij, or Song of Cherubim', in Bowring, I, 157.

Khersonida

479. 'Address to the Deity', 'Medina', 'Sheik-Huiabas Creed', in
Bowring, I, 147-54.
('Address to the Deity' reprinted in J. PIERPONT, American
First Class Book in Reading and Recitation (Boston, Mass.,
1823, 469-71).

'Pervyi chas goda' (1789)

480. 'The First Hour of the Year', in Brown, 494-5. (Prose
extracts).

'Polnoshch''(1804)

481. 'Midnight Hymn', in Bowring, I, 156.

482. 'Midnight', in Brown, 498.(Prose extracts).

'Sud'ba drevnego mira, ili Vsemirnyi potop' (1789)

483. 'The Fate of the Ancient World, or the Deluge', in Brown,
495-6. (Prose extracts, including all the second half of the
poem).

'Tsarstvo vseobshchei liubvi' (1785)

484. 'The Kingdom of Universal Love', in Brown, 494. (Prose
translation of first two stanzas).

O.N.E.

485. 'Children's Offering on a Parent's Birthday', in Bowring, I,
158.

O.N.E.

486. 'Rules for the Heart and the Understanding', in Bowring, I,
159-61.

487. ALTSHULLER, M.G., 'Semen Bobrov and Edward Young', translated
by G.S. SMITH, RLT, 20/21.

BOGDANOVICH, I.F. (1743-1803)

Dushen'ka (1st complete pub. 1783)

488. 'From the Dushenka', in Bowring, I, 165-7 (2 extracts).

489. 'Psyche', translated by L. WIENER, in Wiener, I, 374-7 (Prose translation of excerpts).

490. 'Dushen'ka: An Ancient Tale in Free Verse', translated by H. SEGEL, in Segel, II, 182-238.

491. 'Dushenka', in Brown, 308-10 (Prose extracts).

'Pesnia' ('Piatnadtsat' mne minulo let') (1st pub. 1773)

492. 'The Inexperienced Shepherdess', in Bowring, I, 168-70.

Suguboe blazhenstvo (1765)

493. 'Doubled Happiness', in Brown, 302 (Two extracts).

O.N.E.

494. 'Song from the Old Russian' ('Hark! those tones of music stealing'), in Bowring, I, 171.

O.N.E.

495. 'Song from the Old Russian' ('What to the maiden has happened'), in Bowring, I, 172-4.

BOLOTOV, A.T.   (1738-1833)

Zapiski A.T. Bolotova (1st pub. 1870-3)

496. 'A Contemporary Noble Writes about Pugachev', translated by P. DUKES, in Dukes, I, 132-5.
(From Zapiski A.T. Bolotova, III (St Petersburg, 1873), 376-8, 440-41, 486-91, as reprinted in Khrestomatiia po istorii SSSR: XVIIIv., edited by L.G. Beskrovnyi and B.B. Kafengauz (Moscow, 1963), 411-16).

497. RAEFF, M., 'Introduction', in A.T. Bolotov, Zhizn' i prikliucheniia, I(reprint, Cambridge, 1974), vi-xi.

498. RICE, J.L., 'The Bolotov Papers and Andrei Timofeevich Bolotov, Himself', RR, XXXV, 2(1976), 125-54.

499. RICE, J.L., 'The Memoirs of A.T. Bolotov and Russian Literary History', in Cross, 17-44.

BOLTIN, I.N. (1735-92)

500. ROGGER, H., 'The "Nationalism" of Ivan Nikitič Boltin', in For Roman Jakobson (The Hague, 1956), 423-9.

501. LIPSKI, A., 'Boltin's Defence of Truth and Fatherland', California Slavic Studies, II(1963), 39-52.

BUZHINSKII, G. (?-1731)

Slovo na godovshchinu smerti Petra Velikogo

502. 'An Anniversary Sermon on the Death of... Peter the Great' (Latin and English texts, with related correspondence), translated by T. CONSETT, in his The Present State and Regulation of the Church of Russia, II (1729), 431-40. Reprint, see No. 406.

CATHERINE II, EMPRESS (1729-96)

Memoirs (pub.1859)

503. Memoirs of the Empress Catherine II, Written by Herself, with a Preface by A. HERZEN, translated from the French (1859).

504. Memoirs of Catherine the Great, translated by K. ANTHONY from the German edition (New York, 1935; 1st edition, 1927).

505. The Memoirs of Catherine the Great, edited by D. MAROGER, with an Introduction by G.P. GOOCH, translated from the French by M. BUDBERG (1955).

Nakaz... (1767)

506. 'The "Nakaz" of Catherine the Great', in Dukes, II, 42-129. (Previously unpublished eighteenth-century translation by an unknown hand, c.1767).

O vremia! (1772)

507. 'O Tempora', translated by L. WIENER, in Wiener, I, 272-6. (Act I, Scene 1).

Russkie poslovitsy

508. 'Choice Russian Proverbs', in PRR, 636-7.

'Skazka o tsareviche Khlore' (1782)

509. Ivan Czarowitz, Or the Rose without Prickles that Stings Not (1793). (Translated by M. GUTHRIE(?)). Reprinted in Wiener, I, 276-87.

Vsiakaia vsiachina (1769)

510. 'From "All Kinds of Things"', in Wiener, I, 328-31.

511. ANON., Review of Ivan Czarowitz..., The Analytical Review, XIX(1794), 303.

512. ANON., Review of Ivan Czarowitz..., The Critical Review; or Annals of Literature, XIII(1795), 230-1.

513. ANON., Review of Théâtre de l'Hermitage de Catherine II (2 vols, Paris, 1799), The Critical Review; or Annals of Literature, NS XXVI(1799), 512-16.

514. ANON., Review of Théâtre de l'Hermitage de Catherine II (2 vols, Paris, 1799), Monthly Review, XXVIII(1799), 501-10. (Includes a translation of one scene from Catherine's play La Rage aux Proverbes, pp. 502-5).

515. ANON., Review of Catherine II, Drey Lustspiele, wider Schwärmerey und Aberglauben (Berlin, 1788), The German Museum, I(1800), 570-1.

516. [TURNER, C.E.], 'Studies in Modern Russian Literature. III— Catherine the Second', The Reader, VII(1866), 988-9. (Includes a translation of Act I, Scene 4 of Imeniny gospozhi Vorchalkinoi). Reprinted in Fraser's Magazine, NS XV(1877), 689-94.

517. MARCHANT, F.B., Review of 'The Works of Catherine II. Vol.I. Edited by A.N. PYPIN', Anglo-Russian Literary Society Proceedings, 68(1913), 77-8.

518. SIMMONS, E.J., 'Catherine the Great and Shakespeare', PMLA, XLVII, 3(1932), 790-806.

519. SHMURLO, E., 'Catherine II and Radishchev', SEER, XVII (1939), 618-22.

520. SIMMONS, R.W., jr, 'Catherine II: The Stimulation of Literature by Royal Decree', Kentucky Foreign Language Quarterly, IX, 1(1962), 52-7.

521. McCONNELL, A., 'The Empress and her Protégé: Catherine II and Radishchev', Journal of Modern History, XXXVI(1964), 14-27.

522. BUTLER, W.E., 'The Nakaz of Catherine the Great', American Book Collector, XV, 5(1966), 1-10.

523. BRECHKA, F.T., 'Catherine the Great: The Books She Read', Journal of Library History, IV, 1(1969), 39-51.

524. PERMENTER, H.R., 'The Personality and Cultural Interests of the Empress Catherine II as Revealed in her Correspondence with Friedrich Melchior Grimm' (Ph.D., University of Texas, 1969).

525. PETSSCHAUER, P., 'The Education and Development of an Enlightened Absolutist: The Youth of Catherine the Great, 1729-1762' (Ph.D., New York University, 1969).

526. PETSSCHAUER, P., 'Enlightened Mentors of Catherine the Great', Enlightenment Essays, II(1971), 167-75.

527. CROSS, A.G., 'A Royal Blue Stocking: Catherine the Great's Early Reputation in England as an Authoress', in Gorski vijenats: A Garland of Essays Offered to Professor Elizabeth Mary Hill, edited by R. AUTY et alii (Cambridge, 1970), 85-99.

528. HILLES, F.W., 'Sir Joshua and the Empress Catherine', in Eighteenth-Century Studies in Honor of Donald F. Hyde (New York, 1970), 267-77.

529. GUKOVSKII, G.A., 'The Empress as Writer', in Catherine the Great: A Profile, edited by M. RAEFF (1972), 64-89.

530. LENTIN, A., 'Catherine the Great and Denis Diderot', HT, XXII, 5(1972), 313-20.

531. LENTIN, A., 'Introduction', in Voltaire and Catherine the Great: Selected Correspondence (Cambridge, 1974), 4-32.

532. RAEFF, M., 'The Empress and the Vinerian Professor: Catherine II's Projects of Government Reforms and Blackstone's Commentaries', OSP, NS VII(1974), 17-41.

533. HOME, R.W., 'The Scientific Education of Catherine the Great', MSIS, 11(1976), 18-22.

534. HADLEY, M., 'The Sublime Housewife: An 18th-Century German View of Catherine the Great', Germano-Slavica, II, 3(1977), 181-8.

535. McKENNA, K.J., 'Catherine the Great's Vsiakaia vsiachina and the Spectator Tradition of the Satirical Journal of Morals and Manners' (Ph.D., University of Colorado, 1977).

536. RASMUSSEN, K., 'Catherine II and the Image of Peter I', SR, XXXVII, 1(1978), 51-69.

537. SMITH, G.S., 'Catherine the Great or Katerina the Ingrate? A Little Known English View of the Empress', SGECRN, 6(1978), 57-9.

538. JONES, W.G., '"C'est un fanatique". Catherine II's Judgement on Novikov', SGECRN, 7(1979), 32-3.

539. KAMENDROWSKY, V., 'Catherine II's Nakaz, State Finances and the Encyclopédie', CSS, XIII, 4(1979), 545-54.

540. VON HERZEN, M., 'Catherine II—Editor of Vsiakaia vsiachina? A Reappraisal', RR, XXXVIII, 3(1979), 283-97.

541. KEY, M.R., Catherine the Great's Linguistic Contribution (Carbondale and Edmonton, 1980). (Current Inquiry into Language and Linguistics, No.36).

542. TUMINS, V.A., 'Catherine II, Frederick II and Gustav II: Three Enlightened Monarchs and their Impact on Literature', Transactions of the Fifth International Congress of the Enlightenment, I(Oxford, 1980), 350-6.

543. BARTLETT, R.P., 'Catherine II, Voltaire and Henry IV of France', SGECRN, 9(1981), 41-50.

544. GRIFFITHS, D.M., 'Castéra-Tooke: the First Western Biographer(s) of Catherine II', SGECRN, 10(1982), 50-61.

CHULKOV, M.D. (1743-92)

Gor'kaia uchast' (1789)

545. 'A Bitter Fate', translated by W.E. HARKINS, in Segel, II, 69-75.

Prianichnaia moneta; Dragotsennaia shchuka (from Peresmeshnik)

546. 'Two Stories from The Mocker', translated by J. GOODLIFFE, RLT, 20/21.

Prigozhaia povarikha (1770)

547. 'The Comely Cook, or the Adventures of a Debauched Woman', translated by V. VON WIREN and H. SEGEL, in Segel, II, 28-68.

'Stikhi na kacheli' (1769)

548. 'Verses at the Merry-go-Round', in Brown, 190-3 (extracts).

549. GARRARD, J.G., 'Narrative Technique in Chulkov's Prigozhaia povarikha', SR, XXVII, 4(1968), 554-63.

550. GARRARD, J.G., 'The Portrayal of Reality in the Prose Fiction of M.D. Chulkov', SEER, XLVIII(1970), 16-26.

551. GARRARD, J.G., Mixail Čulkov: An Introduction to his Prose and Verse (The Hague, 1970). Review: J.L. RICE, SEEJ, XV, 4 (1971), 495-501.

552. TITUNIK, I.R., 'Mikhail Chulkov's "Double-Talk" Narrative (Skazka o rozhdenii taftianoi mushki)', CSS, IX, 1(1976), 30-42.

553. OINAS, F.J., 'The Transformation of Folklore into Literature', in American Contributions to the Eighth International Congress of Slavists, II. Literature, edited by V. TERRAS (Columbus, 1978), 576-83.

554. LEVITSKY, A., 'Mikhail Chulkov's The Comely Cook: The Symmetry of a Hoax', in RLT, 20/21.

DANILOV, M.V. (1722-1790?)

Zapiski (1st pub.1842)

555. 'From His "Memoirs"', in Wiener, I, 269-71.

DASHKOVA, E.R. (1743-1810)

Memoirs (1st pub.No.556)

556. Memoirs of the Princess Daschkow, Lady of Honour to Catherine II Empress of All the Russias: Written by Herself: comprising Letters of the Empress, and other Correspondence. Edited from the Originals, by Mrs W. Bradford (2 vols, 1840).

557. The Memoirs of Princess Dashkov, Translated and edited by K. FITZLYON (1958).

558. LONGMIRE, R.A., 'Princess Dashkova and the Cultural Life of 18th Century Russia' (M.A., University of London, 1955).

559. LENTIN, A., 'The Princess Dashkova', HT, XVIII, 12(1968), 823-6; XIX, 1(1969), 18-24.

DENISOV, S. (1682?-1740)

560. SULLIVAN, J., 'Manuscript Copies of Simeon Denisov's The Russian Vineyard', SEER, LVIII(1980), 182-94.

561. SULLIVAN, J., 'Vertograd dukhovnyy: An Extended Edition of Simeon Denisov's Vinograd rossiyskiy', SEER, LVIII(1980), 500-23.

DERZHAVIN, G.R. (1743-1816)

'Blagodarnost' Felitse' (1783)

562. 'Gratitude to Felitsa', translated by C.F. COXWELL, in his
Russian Poems (1929), 32-3.

'Bog' (1784)

563. 'God', in Bowring, I, 3-9 (slightly altered in 2nd ed.).
Reprinted: Monthly Magazine, LI, 1(1821), 132 (extracts);
Eclectic Review, NS XV(1821), 287-8; in J. PIERPONT, American
First Class Book... (Boston, Mass., 1823), 475-8; A. HALL,
Literary Reader (Boston, Mass., 1851), 406-8; E. SARGENT,
Standard Fifth Reader (Boston, Mass., 1856), 153-5; G.S.
HILLIARD, Sixth Reader (Boston, Mass., 1865), 372-3;
M. WILLSON, United States Series (New York, 1872), 364
(fragment); C.W. SANDERS, Fifth Reader (New York, 1868),
162-5; W. FETLER, The Stundist in Siberian Exile and Other
Poems (1922), 21-4.

564. 'To God', in Lewis, 66-72.

565. 'Ode to the Deity', translated by J.K. STALLYBRASS, The
Leisure Hour, 2 May 1870.
Reprinted in Wiener, I, 379-82.

566. 'From the Ode, "God"', translated by C.F. COXWELL, in his
Russian Poems (1929), 29 (Fragment).

567. 'God', in TRL, 46 (Fragment).

568. 'Ode to God', in O. DEACON, Before the Iron Curtain. A
Selection of Russian Verse (Ilfracombe, 1951), 61-4.

569. 'God', in Segel, II, 282-5.

'Derevenskaia zhizn'' (1802)

570. 'Country Life', in Segel, II, 314.

571. 'Country Life', in B. RAFFEL, Russian Poetry under the Tsars
(Albany, 1971), 22.

'Evgeniiu. Zhizn' zvanskaia' (1807)

572. 'To Eugene. Life at Zvanka', in Brown, 402-3 (Prose extracts).

'Felitsa' (1782)

573. 'Felitsa', in Wiener, 385-90 (Prose translation).

574. 'Ode to the Wise Princess Felitsa of the Kirghiz-Kazakh
Horde, Written by a Certain Murza, Long a Resident of Moscow,
but Now living in St. Petersburg Because of his Affairs,
1782', in Segel, II, 270-9.

575. 'Ode to Felitsa', in Brown, 391-2. (Prose extracts).

'Grom' (1806)
576. 'The Storm', in Lewis, 54-5.
Reprinted in Wiener, I, 391-2.

'Kliuch' (1779)

577. 'The Spring', in Brown, 387. (Prose extracts).

'K pervomu sosedu' (1780)
578. 'To a Neighbour', in Bowring, II, 17-20.
Reprinted in F.R. GRAHAME, The Progress of Science... (1865)
(No. 66 above), 107-8.

'Na ptichku' ('Poimali ptichku golosistu') (1792 or 1793)
579. 'Plaint', in TRL, 46.

'Na konchinu grafa Orlova' (1796)
580. 'On the Death of Count Orlov', in Bowring, I, 43.

'Na ot"ezd imperatora...' (1812)
581. 'On the Emperor's Departure, December 7, 1812', translated
by B. DEUTSCH, in A Treasury of Russian Verse, edited by
A. YARMOLINSKY (New York, 1949), 31.

'Na smert' Kateriny Iakovlevny, 1794 godu iiulia 15 dnia
prikliuchivshuiusia'
582. 'On the Death of Katerina Iakovlevna', in Brown, 401.
(Prose).

'Na smert' kniazia Meshcherskogo' (1779)
583. 'On the Death of Meshchersky', in Bowring, I, 10-14.
Reprinted: Monthly Magazine, LI, 1(1821), 132 (extracts).

584. 'On the Death of Prince Meshcherskii', in Segel, II, 257-9.

585. 'Ode on the Death of Prince Meshchersky', in Brown, 387-8.
(Prose extracts).

'Osen' vo vremia osady Ochakova' (1778)
586. 'Autumn during the Siege of Ochakov', in Brown, 395-6.
(Prose extracts).

'Pamiatnik' (1795)

587. 'The Monument', in <u>Segel</u>, II, 308-9.

588. 'Monument', in <u>Brown</u>, 400 (Prose extracts).

'Pavlin' (1795)

589. 'The Peacock', in <u>Brown</u>, 405 (Prose extracts).

'Pchelka' (1796)

590. 'Song', in <u>Bowring</u>, I, 44.

591. 'The Little Bee', translated by C.F. COXWELL, in his <u>Russian Poems</u> (1929), 31-2.

'Potoplenie' (1796)

592. 'The Shipwreck', in <u>Bowring</u>, II, 21.
      Reprinted, without acknowledgement, in <u>Selections from Russian Poetry</u>, selected and compiled by Dr A.S. RAPPOPORT (1907?), 22.

'Priglashenie k obedu' (1795)

593. 'Invitation to Dinner', in <u>Segel</u>, II, 305-7.

594. 'Invitation to Dinner', in <u>Brown</u>, 401 (Prose extracts).

'Reka vremen...' (1816)

595. 'The Stream of Time', translated by J. POLLEN, in his <u>Rhymes from the Russian</u> (1891).
      Reprinted in J. POLLEN, <u>Russian Songs and Lyrics</u> (1916), 112; and in <u>Wiener</u>, I, 392.

596. 'Time's Long and Ever-flowing River', translated by B.DEUTSCH, in <u>A Treasury of Russian Verse</u>, edited by A. YARMOLINSKY (New York, 1949), 31.

597. 'Time's River in its Ceaseless Coursing', in <u>Segel</u>, II, 317.

598. 'Time's Unending River: A Fragment', in B. RAFFEL, <u>Russian Poetry under the Tsars</u> (Albany, 1971), 25.

'Lebed'' (1808)

599. 'The Swan', in B. RAFFEL, <u>Russian Poetry under the Tsars</u> (Albany, 1971), 23-4.

'Solovei vo sne' (1797)

600. 'A Dream of a Nightingale', translated by C.F. COXWELL, in his <u>Russian Poems</u> (1929), 31.

601. 'A Nightingale in a Dream', in Segel, II, 311-12.

602. 'A Dream Nightingale', in B. RAFFEL, <u>Russian Poetry under the Tsars</u> (Albany, 1971), 21.

'Stikhi na rozhdenie v Severe Porfironosnogo otroka' (1779)

603. 'Verses on the Birth in the North of a Porphyrogennete Child'
     in Brown, 393-4 (Prose extracts).

'Tsyganskaia pliaska' (1805)

604. 'The Gypsy Woman's Dance', in Segel, II, 315-16.

'Videnie murzy' (1783-4?)

605. 'The Dream of Myrza', translated by W. TOOKE from the German
     version by A. KOTZEBUE, in H. STORCH, The Picture of
     Petersburg (1801), 390-6 (No. 51).

'Vlastiteliam i sudiiam' (1780?)

606. 'The Lord and the Judge', in Bowring, I(2nd ed. only), 41-2.
     A different version from the 1st edition of Bowring, where
     the poem is attributed to Lomonosov.
     Reprinted, Monthly Magazine, LI, 1(1821), 133 (attributed to
     Lomonosov); J. PIERPONT, American First Class Book...
     (Boston, 1823), 93 (attributed to Lomonosov).

607. 'To Rulers and Judges', in Segel, II, 261.

608. 'To Potentates and Judges', in Brown, 389 (Prose extracts).

'Vodopad' (1791-1794)

609. 'The Waterfall', in Bowring, I, 15-40.
     Reprinted, J. PIERPONT, American First Class Book... (Boston,
     1823), 366-7 (extracts); in Wiener, I, 390-1 (extracts).

610. 'The Waterfall', translated by C.F. COXWELL, in his Russian
     Poems (1929), 29-30.

611. 'The Waterfall', in Segel, II, 287-303.

612. 'The Waterfall', in Brown, 397-9 (Prose extracts).

O.N.E.

613. 'The Empress Approaches Kazan, 1767', translated by C.F.
     COXWELL, in his Russian Poems (1929), 33 (A six-line
     fragment).

O.N.E.

614. 'Fragment' ('The Ass that Looks upon the Stars'), in Bowring,
     II, 22.
     Reprinted in F.R. GRAHAME, The Progress of Science... (1865)
     (No. 66), 106-7.

O.N.E.

615. 'Song' ('How blest am I thy Charms enfolding'), in Lewis, 63.

O.N.E.

616. 'Song' ('The Shades of Spring's Delicious Even'), in Lewis,
     62-3.

O.N.E.

617. 'Song' ('Sweetly Came the Morning Light'), in <u>Lewis</u>, 60-1.

O.N.E.

618. 'Time', in <u>Lewis</u>, 57-9.

O.N.E.

619. 'To Mary' ('Vainly, Mary, dost thou Pray me'), in <u>Lewis</u>, 64-5.

O.N.E.

620. 'To my Heart', in <u>Lewis</u>, 55-6.

621. TURNER, C.E., 'Studies in Russian Literature. VI. Derzhavin', <u>Fraser's Magazine</u>, NS XVI(1877), 45-53.

622. FREELOVE, W., 'Note on English Translators of Derzhavin', <u>Notes and Queries</u>, 6th series (3 July 1880), 15; (25 September 1880), 254.

623. HEDRICK, H.R., 'The Poetry of Deržavin' (Ph.D., Princeton University, 1966).

624. CLARDY, J.V., <u>G.R. Derzhavin: A Political Biography</u> (The Hague-Paris, 1967).

625. HARRIS, J.G., 'The Creative Imagination in Evolution: A Stylistic Analysis of G.R. Derzhavin's Panegyric and Meditative Odes (1774-94)' (Ph.D., Columbia University, 1969).

626. HARVIE, J.A., 'The River of Time', <u>New Zealand Slavonic Journal</u>, III(1969), 54-66.

627. HART, P.R., 'Deržavin's Ode <u>God</u> and the Great Chain of Being', <u>SEEJ</u>, XIV, 1(1970), 1-10.

628. HART, P.R., 'Life against Death in Derzhavin's Odes', <u>CSS</u>, 5, 1(1971), 22-34.

629. SPRINGER, A.R., 'The Public Career and Political Views of G.R. Derzhavin' (Ph.D., University of California at Los Angeles, 1971).

630. HART, P.R., 'Mirza and Mistress in Derzhavin's "Felitsa" Poetry', <u>SR</u>, XXXI, 3(1972), 583-91.

631. HART, P.R., 'Aspects of the <u>Anacreontea</u> in Derzhavin's Verse', <u>SEEJ</u>, XVII, 4(1973), 375-89.

632. HART, P.R., 'Frederick II's <u>Poésies Diverses</u> as a Source for Gavriil Derzavin's Early Odes', <u>Germano-Slavica</u>, 2(1973), 19-27.

633. SHAW, S., 'The Quest for "pokoi" in Derzhavin's Poetry, with Some Reference to Horace', New Zealand Slavonic Journal, II (1973), 133-44.

634. WORTMAN, R., 'Gavrila Romanovich Derzhavin and his Zapiski', in G.R. DERZHAVIN, Zapiski (Reprint, Cambridge, 1973), 1-8. |

635. BAILEY, L.F., 'Consonant Variance in Deržavin's Rhymes: A Preliminary Study' (Ph.D., University of Wisconsin, Madison, 1974).

636. HARVIE, J.A., 'A Note on Derzhavin's Ode to God', MSlS, IX-X (1975), 112-20.

637. HARVIE, J.A., 'In Defence of Derzhavin's Plays', New Zealand Slavonic Journal, NS 2(1975), 1-15.

638. SMITH, G.S., 'G.R. Derzhavin: A Concise Bibliography of Works Published Outside the USSR', SGECRN, 3(1975), 52-6.

639. SPRINGER, A., 'Gavriil Derzhavin's Jewish Reform Project of 1800', CSS, X, 1(1976), 1-23.

640. WATTS, T.J., 'G.R. Derzhavin's Path to the Pre-Romantic Lyric' (Ph.D., New York University, 1976).

641. HARVIE, J.A., 'The Unknown Derzhavin', MSlS, 12(1977), 23-33.

642. HART, P.R., G.R.Derzhavin: A Poet's Progress (Columbus, 1978).

643. HART, P.R., 'Solar Splendor in Russian Verse', in Helios: From Myth to Solar Energy: Images of the Sun in Myth and Legend. A Symposium (New York, 1978), 110-18.

644. VICKERY, W., 'Deržavin's "Na smert' Kateriny Jakovlevny": A Metrical-Stylistic Study', International Journal of Slavic Linguistics and Poetics, XXIII(1981), 163-80.

DESNITSKII, S.E. (1740?-89)

Predstavlenie o uchrezhdenii zakonodatel'noi, suditel'noi i nakazatel'noi vlasti v rossiiskoi imperii (1768)

645. 'Proposal for the Establishment of Legislative, Judicial and Executive Power in the Russian Empire', translated by P.DUKES, in Dukes, I, 47-65.

646. BROWN, A.H., 'The Father of Russian Jurisprudence: The Legal Thought of S.E. Desnitskii', in Russian Law: Historical and Political Perspectives, edited by W.E. BUTLER (Leyden, 1977), 117-41.

DMITRIEV, I.I. (1760-1837)

'Akh! kogda b ia prezhde znala'(pub. 1792)

647. 'O had I but known before', in <u>Bowring</u>, II, 51-2.

648. 'Peasant Woman's Song', in <u>Brown</u>, 513 (Prose version).

'Chizhik i ziablitsa' (1793)

649. 'The Siskin and the Chaffinch', in <u>Russian Lyrics in English Verse</u>, translated by C.T. WILSON (1887), 10-11.

<u>Chuzhoi tolk</u> (1794)

650. 'What Others Say', in <u>Wiener</u>, I, 436-40 (Prose).

651. 'Other Folk's Chatter', in <u>Brown</u>, 525-6 (Prose extracts).

'Dub i trost' (1795)

652. 'The Oak and the Reed', in <u>Brown</u>, 519 (Prose version).

'Epigramma' ('Ia razorilsia ot vorov!') (pub. 1803)

653. 'Epigram', in <u>TRL</u>, 47.

<u>Ermak</u> (1794)

654. 'Jermak', in <u>Bowring</u>, II, 25-34.

655. 'Ermak', in W.H. SAUNDERS, <u>Poetical Translations from the Russian Language</u> (1826), 7-16.

656. 'Yermak', in <u>Russian Lyrics in English Verse</u>, translated by C.T. WILSON (1887), 2-9.
Reprinted in <u>Wiener</u>, I, 431-6.

'Gimn vostorgu' (1792)

657. 'Hymn to Rapture', in <u>Brown</u>, 512 (Prose version).

'Gorlitsa i prokhozhii' (?)

658. 'The Dove and the Stranger', in <u>Bowring</u>, I, 126 (Not in 2nd edition).

'Grust'' (1803)

659. 'Grief', in <u>Brown</u>, 515 (Prose version).

'Ia mos'koi byt' zhelaiu' (1796)

660. 'I would be a Pug-dog', in <u>Brown</u>, 514 (Prose version).

'Iunost', iunost'! veselisia' (pub. 1795)

661. 'Counsel', in <u>Lewis</u>, 38-9.

'K Khloe'(pub. 1792)

662. 'To Chloe', in _Bowring_, II, 55-6.

'Kniga "Razum"' (1803)

663. 'The Book of Reason', in _Brown_, 520.

'K Volge' (1794)

664. 'To the Volga', in _Bowring_, II, 44-8.

'Liubov' i druzhestvo' (1788)

665. 'Love and Friendship', in _Bowring_, I, 127.

'Mesiats' (1805)

666. 'The Moon', translated by W.H. LEEDS, in his 'Russian Fabulists, with Specimens', _Fraser's Magazine_, XXV(1842), 250.

'Mne lekar' govoril: "Net, ni odnoi bol'noi..."' (pub. 1791)

667. 'The Doctor', in _Russian Lyrics in English Verse_, translated by C.T. WILSON (1887), 11.

'Nadgrobie' (1803)

668. 'Over the Grave of Bogdanovich, Author of the Beautiful Poem Psyche', in _Bowring_, I, 126.

'Naslazhdenie' (pub. 1792)

669. 'Enjoyment', in _Bowring_, II, 49-50.

'Nastroiv tomnu liru' (1795)

670. 'Having tuned my languid lyre', in _Brown_, 514 (Prose version).

'Osvobozhdenie Moskvy' (1795)

671. 'Moscow Rescued', in _Bowring_, II, 35-43.
Reprinted, without acknowledgement, in _Selections from Russian Poetry_, selected and compiled by Dr A.S. RAPPOPORT (1907?), 23-30.

'Pchela, shmel' i ia' (1792)

672. 'The Bee, the Bumble-Bee and I', in _Brown_, 518 (Prose version).

'Puteshestvie' (1803)

673. 'The Traveller', in _Brown_, 520 (Prose version).

'Razbitaia skripka' (pub. 1805)

674. 'The Broken Fiddle', in _Bowring_, I, 125.

'Razmyshlenie po sluchaiu groma' (pub. 1805)

675. 'During a Thunder-Storm', in Bowring, I, 119-20.
Reprinted in J. PIERPONT, American First-Class Book...
(Boston, Mass., 1823), 96; and in Wiener, I, 430-31.

'Stonet sizyi golubochek' (pub. 1792)

676. 'Once a gentle turtle dove', in Bowring, II, 53-4.

677. 'The Little Dove', in Lewis, 51-2.
Reprinted in Wiener, I, 429-30.

✓ 'Tsar' i dva pastukha'(pub. 1802)

678. 'The Tzar and the Two Shepherds', in Bowring, I, 121-4.

O.N.E.

679. 'Sympathy', in Russian Lyrics in English Verse, translated
by C.T. WILSON (1887), 11.

O.N.E.

680. 'Laura's Prayer', in Lewis, 53-4.

O.N.E.

681. 'Poets', in TRL, 47.

682. SWIDZINSKA, H., 'I.I. Dmitriev: A Classicist and a
Sentimentalist in the Context of the World and Russian Fable'
(Ph.D., University of Pittsburgh, 1972).

683. CROSS, A.G., 'The Reluctant Memoirist', in I.I. DMITRIEV,
Vzgliad na moiu zhizn' (reprint, Cambridge, 1974), i-xii.

684. CROSS, A.G., 'Dmitriev and Gessner', SGECRN, 2(1974), 32-9.

DOLGORUKAIA, N.B. (1714-71)

Svoeruchnye zapiski (1767)

685. 'From her "Memoirs"', in Wiener, I, 234-41.

686. The Memoirs of Natal'ja Borisovna Dolgorukaja, translated by
C.E. TOWNSEND (Columbus, 1977).
The translation is on pp.33-85, en regard with the original;
the introductory matter discusses the historical, biographical
and linguistic background of the Memoirs.

DZHUNKOVSKII, S.S. (1762-1839)

687. CROSS, A.G., 'Dzhunkovskii's Aleksandrova: Putting Samborskii
in the Picture', SGECRN, 3(1975), 22-9.

EMIN, F.A. (1735?-70)

Adskaia pochta (1769)

688. 'From "Hell's Post"', in Wiener, I, 335-6.

Pis'ma Ernesta i Doravry (1766)

689. 'The Letters of Ernst and Doravra', in Segel, II, 19-25.

690. GARRETSON, D.A., 'Compound Words in the Prose of F.A. Emin:
An Historical Study' (Ph.D., New York University, 1975).

691. BUDGEN, D.E., 'Fedor Emin and the Beginnings of the Russian
Novel', in Cross, 67-94.

692. BUDGEN, D.E., 'The Works of F.A. Emin (1735-70): Literary and
Intellectual Transitions in Eighteenth-Century Russia'
(D.Phil., Oxford University, 1976).

693. ZIELINSKI-SORGENTE, W., 'An Epistolary Novel Re-Evaluated:
The Letters of Ernest and Doravra, by F.A. Emin' (Ph.D.,
Northwestern University, 1978).

FOLK SONGS: see ANONYMOUS WORKS

FONVIZIN, D.I. (1745-92)

694. Dramatic Works of D.I. Fonvizin, translated by M. KANTOR
(Berne-Frankfurt, 1974).
(The Brigadier, 49-86; The Minor, 87-134; A Good Mentor,
135-9; The Selection of a Tutor, 141-50).

Brigadir (1768?) (see also No. 694)

695. 'The Brigadier's Visit', translated by C.E. BECHHOFFER, in
his A Russian Anthology in English (London-New York, 1917),
255-65 (Part of Act V).

696. 'The Brigadier', in Segel, II, 321-73.

'Chistoserdechnoe priznanie v delakh moikh i pomyshleniiakh'

697. 'An Open-Hearted Confession of my Acts and Thoughts', in
Wiener, I, 351-5.

Nedorosl' (1779) (See also Nos 50, 694, 714)

698. 'The Spoiled Boy. A Russian Comedy, by Fon Vizine', The
Magazine of Foreign Literature, I(1823), 267-74.
A detailed synopsis, with translations of various scenes and
passages.

(<u>Nedorosl'</u>, continued)

699. 'The Minor', in <u>Wiener</u>, I, 342-51 (Act I).

700. 'The Young Hopeful', in <u>Masterpieces of the Russian Drama</u>, translated by G.R. NOYES (New York-London, 1933)

701. 'The Infant', in <u>Four Russian Plays</u>, translated by J. COOPER (Harmondsworth, 1972), 47-124.

<u>Pis'ma</u>

702. 'Letters to Count P.I. Panin, During his First Journey Abroad', in <u>Wiener</u>, I, 355-8.

703. 'Letters from my Second Journey Abroad (1777-1778)', in <u>Segel</u>, I, 304-40.

704. 'Letters from my Third Journey Abroad (1784-1785)', in <u>Segel</u>, I, 341-51.

'Rassuzhdenie o nepremennykh gosudarstvennykh zakonakh' (1780s?)

705. 'A Discourse on Permanent Laws of State', translated by R. HINGLEY, in M. RAEFF, <u>Russian Intellectual History: An Anthology</u> (New York, 1966), 96-105.

'Ta Gio, ili velikaia nauka...' (1779)

706. 'Ta Hsüeh, Or That Great Learning Which Comprises Higher Chinese Philosophy', translated by R. HINGLEY, in M. RAEFF, <u>Russian Intellectual History: An Anthology</u> (New York, 1966), 88-95.

'Voprosy i otvety' (1783)

707. 'Queries and Answers', translated by S. BENTHAM (1783), in K.A. PAPMEHL, 'Samuel Bentham and the <u>Sobesednik</u>, 1783', <u>SEER</u>, XLVI(1968), 212-16.
(Includes Catherine II's 'Questions').

'Vseobshchaia pridvornaia grammatika' (?)

708. 'Universal Courtiers' Grammar', in <u>PRR</u>, 23-7.

'Vybor guvernera' (see also No.694)

709. 'The Choice of a Tutor', in <u>Five Russian Plays, With One from the Ukrainian</u>, translated from the Originals with an Introduction by C.E. BECHHOFER (London-New York, 1916), 79-99.

710. TURNER, C.E., 'Studies in Russian Literature. V. Von Viezin', <u>Fraser's Magazine</u>, NS XVI(1877), 40-5.
(Includes some extracts from <u>The Minor</u>, 43-4).

711. BOWRING, L.B., 'A Russian Traveller's Impressions of France a Hundred Years Ago', <u>Anglo-Russian Literary Society Proceedings</u>, 18(1897), 22-32.

712. BRYNER, C., 'Denis Fon Vizin, Patriot', _Slavia_, XIV(1939), 11-18.

713. KANTOR, M., 'Fonvizin and Holberg: A Comparison of _The Brigadier_ and _Jean de France_', _CSS_, VII, 4(1973), 475-84.

714. CROSS, A.G., 'Fonvizin's _Nedorosl'_: An Overlooked English Critique', _SGECRN_, 5(1977), 27-33. (Refers to No. 698).

715. PATTERSON, D., 'Fonvizin's _Nedorosl'_ as a Russian Representative of the _genre sérieux_', _Comparative Literature Studies_, 14(1977), 196-204.

716. SERMAN, I.Z., 'Fonvizin and Fénelon', translated by G.S. SMITH, _SGECRN_, 5(1977), 33-6.

717. MOSER, C.A., _Denis Fonvizin_ (Boston, Mass., 1979).

GOLOVINA, V.N. (1766-1821)

Memoirs

718. _Memoirs of Countess Golovine, a Lady at the Court of Catherine II_, translated from the French by G.M. FOX-DAVIES (1910).

GRIBOVSKII, A.M. (1766-1833)

719. 'From his "Memoirs"', in _Wiener_, I, 405-11.

IAVORSKII, S. (1658-1722)

720. ŠERECH, J., 'Stefan Yavorsky and the Conflict of Ideologies in the Age of Peter I', _SEER_, XXX(1951), 40-62.

KANTEMIR, A.D. (1708-44)

'Pis'mo Kharitona Makentina...' (1744)

721. 'Letter of Xariton Makentin to a Friend on the Composition of Russian Verse', translated by R. SILBAJORIS, in his _Russian Versification..._ (1968), 81-99. (No. 284)

Satiry

722. Extracts from Satires I, IV, and VIII, translated by C.F. COXWELL, in his Russian Poems (1929), 23-4.

Satira I (1729)

723. 'To My Mind', in Wiener, I, 224-9.

724. 'Satire I: To His Mind: On the Scorners of Learning', translated by J. EYRE, SEER, XXI(1943), 1-5.

725. 'Satire I: To My Mind. On the Detractors of Learning', in Segel, I, 155-63.

726. 'To My Mind', in Brown, 37-8 (Prose extracts).

Satira II (1730)

727. 'Second Satire', in Brown, 40 (Prose extracts).

Satira III (1730)

728. 'Third Satire', in Brown, 44-6 (Prose extracts).

Satira VI (1738)

729. 'On Genuine Happiness', in Brown, 51 (Prose extract).

Satira VII (1739)

730. 'Seventh Satire', in Brown, 52 (Prose extract).

731. TURNER, C.E., 'Studies in Modern Russian Literature. II. Kantemir', The Reader, VII(10 November 1866), 919-20. Includes prose extracts from Satires I, II, and III. Reprinted in revised form, Fraser's Magazine, NS XV(1877), 658-64.

732. EVANS, R.J.M., 'Kantemir as a Westerniser in Russian Eighteenth-Century Literature' (M.A., University of London, 1956).

733. EVANS, R.J.M., 'Antiokh Kantemir and His German Translators', SEER, XXXVI(1957), 150-8.

734. EVANS, R.J.M., 'Antiokh Kantemir and his First Biographer and Translator', SEER, XXXVII(1958), 184-95.

735. EVANS, R.J.M., 'Antiokh Kantemir: A Study of his Literary, Political, and Social Life in England, 1732-8' (Ph.D., University of London, 1960).

736. BOSS, V.J., 'Kantemir and Rolli-Milton's "Il Paradiso Perduto"', SR, XXII, 3(1962), 441-55.

737. REDSTON, D.B., 'Kantemir and his Translations' (Ph.D., Vanderbilt University, 1973).

738. ŠILBAJORIS, R., 'Rhythm and Meaning in Kantemir's "Letter to Prince Nikita Jur'evič Trubeckoj"', SEEJ, XVI, 2(1972), 163-72.

739. REDSTON, D., 'The Translations of Kantemir', Journal of Russian Studies, 33(1977), 33-9.

740. STANCHFIELD, G.V., 'Russian Baroque: A.D. Kantemir' (Ph.D., Florida State University, 1977).

KAPNIST, V.V. (1757-1824)

Iabeda (between 1791 and 1798)
741. 'From "The Pettifoggery"', in Wiener, I, 398-402 (Prose extracts from Act III, Scene 6; Act IV, Scene 6).

'Moemu drugu'
742. 'To My Friend', in Brown, 466 (Prose translation).

'Motylek' (pub. 1796)
743. 'Butterfly', in Brown, 464 (Prose translation).

'Na smert' Iulii' (pub. 1792)
744. 'On Julia's Death', in Bowring, II, 187-8.
Reprinted in F.R. GRAHAME, The Progress of Science, Art and Literature in Russia (1865), 108-9, and in Wiener, I, 404-5.

745. 'On the Death of Julia', in Brown, 465 (Prose translation).

'Oda na rabstvo' (1783)
746. 'Ode to Slavery', in Brown, 458-9 (Prose extracts).

'Obukhovka' (1818)
747. 'Obukhovka', in Wiener, I, 402-4 (Prose translation).

748. 'Obukhovka', in Brown, 469-70 (Prose extracts).

'Oda na smert' Pleniry' (1794)
749. 'Ode on the Death of Plenira', in Brown, 463 (Prose extracts).

'Oda na smert' syna moego' (1784)
750. 'Ode on the Death of my Son', in Brown, 461-2 (Prose extracts).

'Oda na unynie' (pub. 1796)
751. 'Ode to Dejection', in Brown, 463-4 (Prose version).

'Pamiati beresta' (1822)
752. 'To the Memory of a Birch Tree', in Brown, 470-1 (Prose extracts).

753. SWOBODA, V., Review of O. OHLOBLYN, Lyudy staroyi Ukrayiny (Munich, 1959), SEER, LXI(1962), 271-4.

754. EDGERTON, W.B., 'A Textological Puzzle in Kapnist's "Ode on Slavery"', in Serta Slavica in Memoriam Aloisii Schmaus, edited by W. GESEMANN et alii (Munich, 1971), 435-44.

755. EDGERTON, W.B., 'Laying a Legend to Rest: The Poet Kapnist and Ukrainian-German Intrigue', SR, XXX, 3(1971), 551-60.

KARAMZIN, N.M. (1766-1826)

Povesti

756. Russian Tales. By Nicolai Karamsin, translated by J.B. ELRINGTON (1803).
('Lisa', 'Flor Silin', 'Natalia', and 'Julia').
A pirate edition of Feldborg's translation, No.757.

757. Tales, from the Russian of Nicolai Karamsin (1804).
('Lisa', 'Flor Silin', 'Natalia', and 'Julia').
Translated from German by A.A. FELDBORG.

758. Selected Prose of N.M. Karamzin, edited and with an Introduction by H.M. NEBEL, jr (Evanston, 1969).

Aonidy (1797)

759. 'Preface to the Second Book of Aonides', in Nebel, 165-9.

'Bednaia Liza' (1791) (See also Nos. 756, 757).

760. 'Poor Lise', translated by M.G., German Museum, III (Jan-Feb. 1801), 30-8, 116-22.

761. 'Poor Liza', in Wiener, II, 34-7.

762. 'Poor Liza', translated by R. WHITTAKER, in Segel, II, 78-93.

763. 'Poor Liza', in Nebel, 53-71.

764. 'Poor Liza', translated by C.R. PROFFER, in From Karamzin to Bunin: An Anthology of Russian Short Stories (Bloomington, 1969), 53-67.

'Bereg' (1802)

765. 'The Haven', in Bowring, II, 125-6.

766. 'The Shore', in Selections of Russian Poetry, translated by B.A. RUDZINSKY and S. GARDINER (1918), 19.

767. 'The Shore', translated by C.F. COXWELL, in his Russian Poems (1929), 34.

'Chto nasha zhizn'? Roman' (1797)

768. 'What is our life but a novel?', translated by V.E. MARSDEN, Anglo-Russian Literary Society Proceedings, 9(1895), 36.

'Chto nuzhno avtoru?' (1794)

769. 'What does an Author Need?', translated by V. von WIREN, in Segel, I, 426-9.

770. 'What does the Writer Need?', in Nebel, 161-3.

'Chuvstvitel'nyi i kholodnyi' (1803)

771. 'The Emotional and the Cold: Two Characters', in Nebel, 197-214.

'Durnoi vkus' (1799)

772. 'To Nicander', in Bowring, I, 116.

'Epitafiia' (1797)

773. 'He managed to live a long life through', in Bowring, I, 116. (Not in 2nd edition).

'Epitafii' (1792)

774. 'A heavenly soul has returned to heaven', in Brown, 539 (Prose version of Nos. I and V)

'Frol Silin' (1791) (see also Nos 756, 757)

775. 'Flor Silin: A Russian Tale', translated by M.G., German Museum, II (August 1800), 104-6.

Istoriia gosudarstva rossiiskogo (1818-26)

776. 'History of Russia', Penny Magazine, CCXXXV (October-November 1835), 465-72 (Supplement).

777. 'From the "History of the Russian Empire"', in Wiener, II, 37-40. (The Introduction).

778. 'Foreword to History of the Russian State', translated by J. PELENSKI, in M. RAEFF, Russian Intellectual History: An Anthology (New York, 1966), 117-24.

779. 'History of the Russian State', translated by H. DEBEVC-MOROZ, in Black, 199-220.

'Iuliia' (See also Nos 756 and 757)

780. 'Julia. Karamsin's Russian Tale', translated by M.G., German Museum, II (September 1800), 211-24. Reprinted: The Universal Magazine (October 1800); Belle Assemblée (February, 1809); The Monthly Pantheon, II(May 1809), 365-74; New London Review, CVII(October 1800), 274-80.

781. Karamsin's Julia translated from the Russ in to the French by Mr du Bouillier and from the French in to the English by Ann P[renser] H[awkins](St Petersburg, 1803).

782. 'Julia', in Nebel, 133-52.

'K D[mitrievu]' (1788)

783. 'To D[mitriev]', in Brown, 531 (Prose version).

'Khloe' (1795)

784. 'Chloe', in Brown, 539 (Prose version).

'Kladbishche' (1792)

785. 'The Churchyard', in Bowring, I, 108-10.
Reprinted: New Edinburgh Review, II, 3(January 1822);
Kaleidoscope, II, 93(9 April 1822), 316; Tickler's Magazine,
IV, 12(1 December 1822), 250; J.PIERPONT, American First
Class Book... (Boston, Mass., 1823), 377-8; Monthly Magazine,
XXV (1838); L. OSGOOD, Progressive Fifth Reader (Pittsburgh,
1858), 210-11; G.S. HILLIARD, Sixth Reader (Boston, Mass.,
1865), 372-3; M. WILLSON, United States Series (New York,
1892), 107-8; Wiener, II, 33-4.

'K milosti' (1792)

786. 'To Mercy', in Brown, 536-7 (Prose extracts).

'K prekrasnoi' (1791)

787. 'To ---', in Bowring, II, 129-30.

'K solov'iu' (1793)

788. 'To the Nightingale', in Bowring, II, 131-2.

'Lettre au Spectateur sur la littérature russe'

789. 'A Few Words about Russian Literature', translated by
V. von WIREN, in Segel, I, 430-41.

'Lileia' (1795)

790. 'Lilea', in Bowring, I, 114-15.
Reprinted: European Magazine, LXXXII(November 1822), 456.

'Mneniia russkogo grazhdanina' (1819)

791. 'Opinion of a Russian Citizen', in F.R. GRAHAME, The Progress
of Science... (1865), 198-201.
Apparently taken from I. GOLOVIN, History of Alexander I
(1858).

792. 'Opinion of a Russian Citizen', translated by J.L. BLACK, in
Black, 193-6.

'Moia ispoved'. Pis'mo k izdateliu zhurnala' (1802)

793. 'My Confession: A Letter to an Editor of a Journal', in <u>Nebel</u>, 171-83.

'Mysli ob istinnoi svobode' (1825)

794. 'Thoughts on True Freedom', translated by H. DEBEVC-MOROZ, in <u>Black</u>, 197-8.

'Natal'ia, boiarskaia doch'' (1792) (See also No.756)

795. 'Natalie, the Boyar's Daughter', in <u>Nebel</u>, 73-116.

'O Bogdanoviche i ego sochineniia' (1803)

796. 'Bogdanovich. Translated from Karamsin's Vestnik', in <u>Bowring</u>, I, 105-16.

'Obshchestvo v Amerike' (1802)

797. 'Society in America', translated by J.L. BLACK, <u>Laurentian University Review</u>, IV, 3(1974), 43-4.

'O knizhnoi torgovle...' (1802)

798. 'Present state of commerce in books, with remarks on the love of reading, in the Interior of Russia', <u>The Literary Panorama</u>, I(1807), 145-8.
[Translated by A.G. EVSTAF'EV].

799. 'The Book Trade and the love of Reading in Russia', translated by J. PELENSKI, in M. RAEFF, <u>Russian Intellectual History: An Anthology</u> (New York, 1966), 113-16.

800. 'On the Book Trade and the Love of Reading in Russia', translated by V. von WIREN, in <u>Segel</u>, I, 449-53.

801. 'On the Book Trade and Love of Reading in Russia', in <u>Nebel</u>, 185-90.

'O liubvi k otechestvu i narodnoi gordosti' (1802)

802. 'Love of Country and National Pride', translated by J. PELENSKI, in M. RAEFF, <u>Russian Intellectual History: An Anthology</u> (New York, 1966), 107-12.

803. 'On Love for the Fatherland and National Pride', translated by V. von WIREN, in <u>Segel</u>, I, 442-8.

'Osen'' (1789)

804. 'Autumn', in <u>Bowring</u>, I, 111-13.
Reprinted, without acknowledgement, in <u>Selections from Russian Poetry</u>, selected and compiled by Dr A.S. RAPPOPORT (1907?), 31-2, as 'The Dry Leaves are Falling'.

805. 'Autumn', in <u>Brown</u>, 533 (Prose version).

'O Shekspire i ego tragedii Iulii Tsezar''

806. 'On Shakespeare and his Tragedy <u>Julius Caesar</u>', in <u>Nebel</u>, 155-60.

'Ostrov Borngol'm' (1794)

807. 'The Island of Bornholm', translated by W.E. HARKINS, in <u>Segel</u>, II, 94-105.

808. 'The Island of Bornholm', in <u>Nebel</u>, 117-31.

'O sluchaiakh i kharakterakh v rossiiskoi istorii...' (1802)

809. 'On Events and Characters in Russian History that are Possible Subjects of Art', translated by V. von WIREN, in <u>Segel</u>, I, 459-69.

'Osvobozhdenie Evropy'(1814)

810. 'Proud city! Sovereign-Mother thou!', in R. LYALL, <u>The Character of the Russians and a Detailed History of Moscow</u> (1823), 514-15.
(Two stanzas from Karamzin's poem, translated by J. BOWRING, but not included in <u>Bowring</u>).

'Otchego v Rossii tak malo avtorskikh talantov?' (1802)

811. 'Why are there so few Talented Authors in Russia?', translated by V. von WIREN, in <u>Segel</u>, I, 454-8.

812. 'Why is there so little Writing Talent in Russia?', in <u>Nebel</u>, 191-6.

'Otstavka' (1796)

813. 'Retirement', in <u>Brown</u>, 540 (Prose version).

'Ten' i predmet'

814. 'The Shadow and the Substance', in <u>Selections of Russian Poetry</u>, translated by B.A. RUDZINSKY and S. GARDINER (1918), 20.

<u>Pis'ma russkogo puteshestvennika</u> (1791)

815. <u>Travels from Moscow through Prussia, Germany, Switzerland, France and England</u>, 3 vols (1803).
(Translated by A.A. FELDBORG from the German version by J. RICHTER).

816. 'Letters of a Russian Traveller', in <u>Wiener</u>, II, 28-33.
(Extracts: '1st Letter'; 'On French Tragedy'; 'On Shakespeare').

817. [3 Letters], in <u>A Russian Anthology in English</u>, edited by C.E. BECHHOFER (London and New York, 1917), 69-81.
(Letters from Weimar, Paris, and London).

818. <u>Letters of a Russian Traveler 1789-1790</u>, translated and abridged by F. JONAS (New York, 1957).
Extracts reprinted in <u>Segel</u>, I, 395-426.

'Pis'mo anglichanina iz Kveveka' (1803)

819. 'An Englishman's Letter from Quebec', translated by
H. DEBEVC-MOROZ, _Laurentian University Review_, IV, 3(1974),
45-6.

'Poslanie k Aleksandru Alekseevichu Pleshcheevu' (1794)

820. 'Epistle to Alexander Alexeevich Pleshcheev', in _Brown_,
537-8 (Prose extracts).

'Poslanie k zhenshchinam' (1795)

821. 'Ah, I did not know thee! (From "A Message to Women")', in
Selections of Russian Poetry, translated by B.A. RUDZINSKY
and S. GARDINER (1918), 17-18.

822. 'I knew thee not', translated by C.F. COXWELL, in his _Russian
Poems_ (1929), 34-5.
(The same extract as No. 821, but a different version).

'Poeziia' (1787)

823. 'Poesy', in _Brown_, 529-30 (Prose extracts).

'Raisa' (1791)

824. 'Raïssa', in _Bowring_, II, 119-24.

'Rytsar' nashego vremeni' (1803)

825. 'A Knight of Our Time', translated by A.G. CROSS, in
RLT, 20/21.

'Zakony osuzhdaiut' (1794)

826. 'The Song of Bornholm', in _Bowring_, I, 105-7.

'Zapiska o drevnei i novoi Rossii' (1811)

827. _Karamzin's Memoir on Ancient and Modern Russia. A Translation
and Analysis_, by R. PIPES (Cambridge, Mass., 1959).

'Zapiska o N.I. Novikove' (1818)

828. 'A Note about N.I. Novikov', translated by V. von WIREN, in
Segel, I, 470-2.

'Zhil-byl v svete dobryi tsar'' (1790)

✓ 829. 'Song of the Good Tsar', in _Bowring_, II, 127-8.

830. ANON., Review of German translation of _Letters of a Russian
Traveller_, _The Anti-Jacobin Review and Magazine_, XI(1802),
500-506.

831. ANON., Review of German translation of _Letters of a Russian
Traveller_, _The German Museum_, II(October 1800), 356.

832. ANON., Review of Russian Tales... (No. 756), The Scots Magazine, LXV(1803), 550.

833. ANON., Review of Russian Tales... (No. 756), The Monthly Review or Literary Journal, XLIV(1804), 262-72.

834. ANON., Review of Russian Tales... (No. 756), Annual Review, and History of Literature, II(1804), 97-100.

835. ANON., Review of Russian Tales... (No. 756), The Anti-Jacobin Review and Magazine, XVII(1804), 23-37.

836. [BROUGHAM, H.], Review of Russian Tales... (No. 756), Edinburgh Review, III(1804), 321-8.

837. ANON., Review of Russian Tales... (No. 756), The Annual Register, or General Repository...for the year 1803(1804),

838. ANON., 'N.M. Karamzin', in The Pantheon of the Age or, Memoirs of 3000 contemporary public characters British and Foreign, of all ranks and professions (1825), 451.

839. WHITEHEAD, S.D., 'Karamzin's History', Foreign Quarterly Review, III(September, 1828), 148-84.

840. BOWRING, J., Autobiographical Recollections of Sir John Bowring (1877), 122-3.

841. TURNER, C.E., 'Studies in Russian Literature. VII. Karamsin', Fraser's Magazine, NS XVI(1877), 186-95.

842. ANON., 'A Great Historian (1766-1826)', Anglo-Russian Literary Society Proceedings, 78(1917), 67-8.

√ 843. PIPES, R., 'Karamzin's Conception of the Monarchy', HSS, IV (1957), 35-58.

844. STILMAN, L., 'Introduction', in N.M. KARAMZIN, Letters of a Russian Traveler (New York, 1957), 3-26 (No. 818).

845. DEWEY, H.W., 'Sentimentalism in the Historical Writings of N.M. Karamzin', in American Contributions to the Fourth International Congress of Slavists (The Hague, 1958), 41-50.

846. McGREW, R.E., 'Notes on the Princely Role in Karamzin's Istorija Gosudarstva Rossijskago', SR, XVIII(1959), 12-24.

847. PIPES, R., 'The Background and Growth of Karamzin's Political Ideas down to 1810', in Karamzin's Memoir... (No.827), 3-100.

848. CROSS, A.G., 'Karamzin and England', SEER, XLIII, 100(1964), 91-114.

849. CROSS, A.G., 'N.M. Karamzin and Barthelémy's Voyage du jeune Anacharsis', MLR, LXI(1966), 467-72.

850. ANDERSON, R.B., 'Evolving Narrative Methods in the Prose of
      N.M. Karamzin' (Ph.D., University of Michigan, 1967).

851. CROSS, A.G., 'Karamzin Studies', SEER, XLV, 104(1967), 1-11.

852. GARRARD, J.G., 'Karamzin in Recent Soviet Criticism: A Review
      Article', SEEJ, XI, 4(1967), 464-72.

853. NEBEL, H.M.jr, N.M. Karamzin: A Russian Sentimentalist (The
      Hague, 1967).

854. CROSS, A.G., 'Problems of Form and Literary Influence in the
      Poetry of Karamzin', SR, XXVII(1968), 39-48.

855. BLACK, J.L., 'The Soviets and the Anniversary of N.M. Karamzin',
      The New Review: A Journal of East-European History, VIII, 3
      (1968), 139-47.

✓856. BLACK, J.L., 'History in Politics: Karamzin's Istoriia as an
      Ideological Catalyst in Russian Society', Laurentian University
      Review, I, 2(1968), 106-13.

857. ANDERSON, R.B., 'The "Split Personality" of the Narrator in
      N.M. Karamzin's Pis'ma russkogo puteshestvennika: A Textual
      Analysis', Études slaves et est-européennes, XIII(1968), 20-31.

858. BLACK, J.L., 'Nicholas Karamzin's Scheme for Russian History',
      in Eastern Europe: Historical Essays (Toronto, 1969), 16-33.

859. CROSS, A.G., 'Karamzin in English: A Review Article', CSS,
      III(1969), 716-27.

860. CROSS, A.G., 'N.M. Karamzin's "Messenger of Europe" (Vestnik
      Evropy), 1802-3', Forum for Modern Language Studies, V(1969),
      1-25.

861. BLACK, J.L., 'N.M. Karamzin, Napoleon, and the Notion of
      Defensive War in Russian History', CSP, XII, 1(1970), 30-46.

862. NEBEL, H.M.jr, 'Introduction', in The Selected Prose of N.M.
      Karamzin (Evanston, 1969), 3-49 (No. 758).
      (Review: J.L. RICE, SEEJ, XIV(1970), 384-8).

863. ANDERSON, R.B., 'Karamzin's Concept of Linguistic
      "Cosmopolitanism" in Russian Literature', Studies by Members
      of SCMLA, XXXI, 4(1971), 168-70.

864. CROSS, A.G., N.M. Karamzin: A Study of his Literary Career
      1783-1803 (Carbondale and Edwardsville, 1971).

865. BLACK, J.L., 'Interpretations of Poland in Nineteenth Century
      Russian Nationalist-Conservative Historiography', The Polish
      Review, XVII, 4(1972), 20-41.

866. COLE, E.A., 'The Enlightened Nationalism of N.M. Karamzin' (Ph.D., University of California at Berkeley, 1972).

867. CROSS, A.G., 'Karamzin's First Short Story?', in Russia: Essays in History and Literature, edited by L.H. LEGTERS (Leiden, 1972), 38-55.

868. DAVIDSON, D.E., 'N.M. Karamzin and German Literature: Antecedents of Russian Romanticism' (Ph.D., Harvard University, 1972).

869. MOCHA, F., 'The Karamzin-Lelewel Controversy', SR, XXXI, 3 (1972), 592-610.

870. ANDERSON, R.B., N.M. Karamzin's Prose. The Teller in the Tale: A Study in Narrative Technique (Houston, 1974).

871. DAVIDSON, D.E., 'N.M. Karamzin and the New Critical Vocabulary: Toward a Semantic History of the Term Romantic in Russia', in Mnemozina. Studia litteraria russica in honorem Vsevolod Setchkarev, edited by J.T. BAUER and N.W. INGHAM (Munich, 1974) 88-94.

872. GARRARD, J.G., 'Karamzin, Mme de Staël, and the Russian Romantics', in American Contributions to the Seventh International Congress of Slavists. II. Literature and Folklore (The Hague, 1974), 221-46.

873. Essays on Karamzin: Russian Man-of-Letters, Political Thinker, Historian, 1766-1826, edited by J.L. BLACK (The Hague-Paris, 1975).

874. ANDERSON, R.B., 'Karamzin's Letters of a Russian Traveller: An Education in Western Sentimentalism', in Black, 22-39.

875. BLACK, J.L., 'The Primečanija: Karamzin as a "Scientific" Historian of Russia', in Black, 127-47.

876. CLARKE, J.E.M., 'Karamzin's Conception of Church Slavonic', SEER, LIII, 133(1975), 493-503.

877. CROSS, A.G., 'Karamzin's Versions of the Idyll', in Black, 75-90.

878. GARRARD, J.G., 'Poor Erast, or Point of View in Karamzin', in Black, 40-55.

879. KISLJAGINA, L.G., 'The Question of the Development of N.M. Karamzin's Social Political Views in the Nineties of the Eighteenth Century: N.M. Karamzin and the Great French Bourgeois Revolution', in Black, 91-104.

880. KOCHETKOVA, N., Nikolay Karamzin (Boston, Mass., 1975).

881. NEUHAUSER, R., 'Karamzin's Spiritual Crisis of 1793 and 1794', in <u>Black</u>, 56-74.

882. ROTHE, H., 'Karamzin and his Heritage: History of a Legend', in <u>Black</u>, 148-90.

883. BLACK, J.L., 'N.M. Karamzin and the Dilemma of Luxury in Eighteenth-Century Russia', <u>Studies on Voltaire and the Eighteenth Century</u>, CLI-CLV(1976), 313-22.

884. CROSS, A.G., 'Whose Initials? Unidentified Persons in Karamzin's Letters from England', <u>SGECRN</u>, 6(1978), 26-36.

885. LITTLE, E., 'The Peasant and the Station Master: A Question of Realism', <u>Journal of Russian Studies</u>, 38(1979), 23-31. (On 'Bednaia Liza').

886. GRIKHIN, V.A., 'Nikolai Karamzin and his Novel, <u>Poor Liza</u>', in N.M. Karamzin, <u>Bednaia Liza</u> (Moscow, 1980), 7-18.

887. CLARKE, J.E.M., 'From the History of Russian Linguistics: Karamzin's Analysis of the Pre-Literary State of the Slavonic Languages', <u>Russian Linguistics</u>, V(1981), 235-43.

888. HAMMARBERG, G., 'Metafiction in Russian 18th Century Prose: Karamzin's <u>Rycar' našego vremeni</u> or <u>Novyj Akteon, vnuk Kadma i Garmonii</u>', <u>Scando-Slavica</u>, 27(1981), 27-46.

889. HAMMARBERG, G.B., 'Karamzin's Prose Fiction: The Poetics of Co-Creation' (Ph.D., University of Michigan, 1982).

KARZHAVIN, E.N. (1745-1812)

890. DVOICHENKO-MARKOV, E., 'A Russian Traveler to Eighteenth-Century America', <u>Proceedings of the American Philosophical Society</u>, XCVII, 4(1953), 350-55.

KHEMNITSER, I.I. (1745-84)

'Bogach i bedniak'(pub.1779)

891. 'The Rich and the Poor Man', in <u>Bowring</u>, I, 139-41. Reprinted: J. PIERPONT, <u>American First Class Book...</u> (Boston, 1823), 378-9.

✓'Dobryi tsar''(pub.1872)

892. 'The Good Tsar', translated by B. COHEN, in <u>Segel</u>, II, 252.

'Dva l'va sosedi'(pub.1873)

893. 'The Two Neighbor Lions', in <u>Brown</u>, 433-4 (Prose translation).

'Khoziain i myshi'(pub.1779)

894. 'Master and Mice', translated by B. COHEN, in Segel, II, 242-3.

'Kon' verkhovyi'(pub. 1779)

895. 'The Riding Horse', in Brown, 434 (Prose translation).

'Kury i galka' (pub.1872)

896. 'The Hens and the Jackdaw-, translated by B. COHEN, in Segel, II, 252-3.

'Lev-svat'(pub.1873)

897. 'The Matchmaker-Lion', translated by B. COHEN, in Segel, II, 250-51.

'Lev, uchredivshii sovet'(pub.1779)

898. 'The Lion's Council of State', in Bowring, I, 142-3. Reprinted in Wiener, I, 306-7.

899. 'The Lion who Created a Council', in Brown, 432-3 (Prose translation).

'Loshad' i osel'(pub.1792)

900. 'The Horse and the Donkey', translated by B. COHEN, in Segel, II, 246.

'Medved'-pliasun'(pub.1779)

901. 'The Dancing Bear', in The Book of the Bear, being Twenty-one tales newly translated from the Russian by Jane Harrison and Hope Mirrlees (1926), 67-9.

902. 'The Dancing Bear', translated by J. EYRE, SEER, XX(1941), 86-7.

'Metafizicheskii uchenik'(pub.1799)

903. 'The Student of Metaphysics', translated by B. COHEN, in Segel, II, 246-8.

'Metafizik'(pub.1873)

904. 'Metaphysics', translated by H.S. EDWARDS, in his The Russians at Home and the Russians Abroad: Sketches, Unpolitical and Political of Russian Life under Alexander II, I(1861), 125-7. Reprinted: F.R. GRAHAME, The Progress of Science... (1865), 109-10.

905. 'The Metaphysician', translated by J. EYRE, SEER, XX(1941), 85-6.

'Muzhik i korova'(pub.1779)

906. 'The Peasant and the Cow', translated by B. COHEN, in Segel, II, 242.

'Oboz' (pub.1779)

907. 'The Waggons', in Bowring, I, 144.

'Pauk i mukhi' (pub.1782)

908. 'The Spider and the Flies', translated by B. COHEN, in Segel, II, 253.

909. 'Spider and Flies: A Fable', in B. RAFFEL, Russian Poetry under the Tsars (Albany, 1971), 19.

'Pes i l'vy' (pub.1873)

910. 'The Dog and the Lions', translated by B. COHEN, in Segel, II, 251-2.

'Popugai' (pub.1782)

911. 'The Parrot', translated by B. COHEN, in Segel, II, 245.

'Privilegiia' (pub.1799)

912. 'Privilege', translated by B. COHEN, in Segel, II, 248-50.

913. 'The Privilege', in Brown, 435-6 (Prose translation).

'Stroitel'' (pub.1779)

914. 'The House-Builder', in Bowring, I, 137-8.
     Reprinted: J. PIERPONT, American First Class Book... (Boston, Mass., 1823), 93-4.

'Umiraiushchii otets' (pub.1779)

915. 'The Dying Father', in Brown, 432 (Prose translation).

'Zelenyi osel' (pub.1782)

916. 'The Green Ass', translated by B. COHEN, in Segel, II, 243-4.

KHERASKOV, M.M. (1733-1807)

'Bogatstvo' (1769)

917. 'Wealth', in Brown, 254-5 (Prose translation).

'Istinnoe blagopoluchie' (1762)

918. 'Genuine Happiness', in Brown, 252.

'K A.A.R.' (1769)

919. 'To A[lexei] A[ndreevich] R[zhevsky]', in Brown, 254 (Prose translation).

'K svoei lire' (1762)

920. 'To My Lyre', in Brown, 252-3 (Prose translation).

<u>Rossiiada</u> (1779)

921. 'Fragments of the Russiad', in <u>Poetical Translations from the Russian Language</u>, by W.H. SAUNDERS (1826), 48-51.

922. 'From the "Rossiad"', in <u>Wiener</u>, I, 218-30 (Prose extracts).

923. 'The Rossiad: An Epic Poem' (Canto I), translated by H. SEGEL, in <u>Segel</u>, II, 110-22.

'Tebe priiazni bole' (1762)

924. 'To You More Pleasing', in <u>Brown</u>, 253 (Prose translation).

'Verbliud i slon' (1764)

925. 'Camel and Elephant', in <u>Brown</u>, 254 (Prose translation).

926. VLASTO, A.P., 'M.M. Heraskov: A Study in the Intellectual Life of the Age of Catherine the Great' (Ph.D., Cambridge University, 1952).

927. VLASTO, A.P., 'A Noble Failure--Kheraskov's <u>Vladimir Vozrozhdyonny</u>, in <u>Gorski vijenats: A Garland of Essays Offered to Professor Elizabeth Mary Hill</u>, edited by R. AUTY et alii (Cambridge, 1970), 276-89.

928. GREEN, M.A., 'Mixail Xeraskov and his Contribution to the Eighteenth Century Russian Theater' (Ph.D., University of California at Los Angeles, 1973).

929. GREEN, M.A., 'Kheraskov and the Christian Tragedy', <u>California Slavic Studies</u>, IX(1976), 1-25.

930. GREEN, M.A., 'Kheraskov's <u>Gonimye</u>: Shakespeare's Second Appearance in Russia', <u>SR</u>, XXXV, 2(1976), 249-57.

931. GREEN, M.A., 'Masonry, Kheraskov and Mozart: A Footnote', <u>SGECRN</u>, 7(1979), 34-7.

932. GREEN, M.A., 'Kheraskov and the Morality Play in Mid-Eighteenth-Century Russia', <u>SGECRN</u>, 9(1981), 21-8.

933. GREEN, M.A., 'Kotzebue and Kheraskov: Sentimentalism in its Pre-Romantic Stage', <u>SGECRN</u>, 10(1982), 20-29.

934. HARVIE, J.A., 'Kheraskov's <u>The Nun of Venice</u>', <u>RLT</u>, 20/21.

KHOVANSKII, G.A. (1767-96)

'Nezabudochka' (1796)

935. 'Through the silent evening hours', in <u>Bowring</u>, II, 235-6.

KNIAZHNIN, Ia.B. (1742-91)

<u>Chudaki</u> (1790)
936. 'Odd People' (Act II, scene 2), in <u>Wiener</u>, I, 311-15.

<u>Didona</u> (1769)
937. 'Dido', in <u>Brown</u>, 331 (Three speeches by Dido).

<u>Neschast'e ot karety</u> (1779)
938. 'The Ill-Fated Coach', translated by J. EYRE, <u>SEER</u>, XXII, 58 (1944), 125-37.

939. 'Misfortune from a Coach', in <u>Segel</u>, II, 376-93.

<u>Vadim novgorodskii</u> (1789)
940. 'Vadim of Novgorod' (Act I, scene 2), in <u>Wiener</u>, I, 309-10.

941. 'Vadim of Novgorod', translated by R.and R. FORTUNE, in <u>RLT</u>, 20/21.

KOMAROV, M. (?-1812)

942. STENBOCK-FERMOR, E., 'The Story of Van'ka Kain and its Ties with Russian Folklore' (Ph.D., Radcliffe College, 1955).

943. TITUNIK, I.R., 'Matvej Komarov's <u>Van'ka Kain</u> and Eighteenth-Century Russian Prose Fiction', <u>SEEJ</u>, XVIII, 4(1974), 351-66.

KOSTROV, E.I. (1755-96)

'K babochke'
944. 'To a Butterfly', in <u>Brown</u>, 481 (Prose translation).

'Kliatva'
945. 'The Vow', in <u>Bowring</u>, I, 181.
     Reprinted: <u>Kaleidoscope</u>, II, 101(4 June 1822), 380.

'Pis'mo k tvortsu ody, sochinennoi v pokhvalu Felitsy, tsarevne Kirgizkaisatskoi'
946. 'Letter to the Creator of the Ode in Praise of "Felitsa, the Kirgiz-Kaysak Princess",' in <u>Wiener</u>, I, 359-61.

947. 'Epistle to the Creator of the Ode Composed in Praise of Felitsa, the Kirgiz-Kaisak Queen', in <u>Brown</u>, 478-9 (Prose extracts).

948. WORTH, D.S., 'Remarks on Eighteenth-Century Russian Rhyme (Kostrov's Translation of the <u>Iliad</u>)', in <u>Slavic Poetics</u>, edited by R. JAKOBSON et alii (The Hague-Paris, 1973), 525-30.

KOTLIAREVSKII, I.P. (1769-1838)

949. MANNING, C.A., 'The Aeneid of Kotliarevsky', Classical Weekly, XXXVI(1942), 91-3.

950. GRAHAM. H.F., 'The Travestied Aeneid and Ivan P. Kotliarevskii, The Ukrainian Vergil', Vergilius, 5(1959), 5-11.

951. ZYLA, W.T., 'A Ukrainian Version of the Aeneid: Ivan Kotliarevskii's Enejida', Classical Journal, LXVII(1972), 193-7.

KRYLOV, I.A. (1768-1844)

'Kaib'(1792)

952. 'Kaïb', in TRL, 30-34.

'Mysli filosofa po mode' (1792)

953. 'Thoughts of a Philosopher à la Mode', in Brown, 566-8 (Extracts).

'Pokhval'naia rech' Ermalafidu'

954. 'Eulogy of Ermalafid', in Brown, 566 (Extracts)

'Pokhval'naia rech' v pamiat' moemu dedushke' (1792)

955. 'Eulogy to the Memory of my Grandfather', translated by P.R. HART, Satire Newsletter, IX(1971), 43-9.

956. 'Eulogy to the Memory of my Grandfather', in Brown, 564-5 (Extracts).

957. REVE, K. van H., 'The Silence of Krylov', in Dutch Contributions to the Fourth International Congress of Slavists (The Hague, 1958), 131-8.

958. STEPANOV, N., Ivan Krylov (New York, 1973).

959. WERCHUN, Z.J., 'The Influence of La Fontaine on Krylov' (Ph.D., Northwestern University, 1973).

960. HART, P.R., 'Ivan Krylov and the Mock Eulogy', Satire Newsletter, IX(1971), 1-5.

LABZINA, A.E. (1758-1828)

961. ZACEK, J.C., 'Introduction', in A.E. LABZINA, Vospominaniia 1763-1819 (Reprint, Cambridge, 1974), i-viii.

LEBEDEV, G.S. (1749-1817)

962. DAS GUPTA, R.K., 'G.S. Lebedev (1749-1817): The First Russian Indologist', <u>OSP</u>, VII(1957), 1-16.

LOMONOSOV, M.V. (1711-65)

<u>Kratkii rossiiskii letopisets s rodosloviem</u>

963. <u>A Chronological Abridgement of the Russian History; Translated From the Original Russian</u> (1767).
[Translated by Georg Forster].

'Oda na den' vosshestviia... Elizavety Petrovny'

964. 'Ode on the Day of the Ascension to the All-Russian Throne of Her Majesty the Empress Elizabeth Petrovna, the Year 1747', in <u>Segel</u>, I, 194-201.

'Oda... na vziatie Khotina' (1739)

965. 'Ode to Her Imperial Majesty the Empress Anne of Russia, on the Victory gained over the Turks and Tartars, and the taking of Khotin, in the year 1739', <u>The Foreign Quarterly Review</u>, I (1827), 628-31.
[Prose translation by I.Ia. SMIRNOV].
Reprinted in F.R. GRAHAME, <u>The Progress of Science...</u> (1865), 45-9; and in <u>Wiener</u>, I, 246-51.

966. 'The Capture of Khotin' (Extracts in verse), translated by C.F. COXWELL, in his <u>Russian Poems</u> (1929), 268-9.

967. 'Ode to Her Majesty the Empress of Blessed Memory Anna Ioannovna on the Victory over the Turks and on the Seizure of Khotin in the Year 1739', in <u>Segel</u>, I, 182-92.

'Oda, v kotoroi ee velichestvu blagodarenie ot sochinitelia prinositsia 1750 goda'

968. 'Ode of 1750', in <u>Brown</u>, 88 (Prose translation of two stanzas).

'Oda, vybrannaia iz Iova'

969. 'Ode from Job', in <u>Bowring</u>, II, 3-9.
Reprinted in F.R. GRAHAME, <u>The Progress of Science...</u> (1865), 42-3; and, without acknowledgement, in <u>Selections from Russian Poetry</u>, selected and compiled by Dr A.S. RAPPOPORT (1907?), 16-21.

970. 'Ode from the Book of Job', in <u>Brown</u>, 89 (Prose translation of four stanzas).

Pis'ma

971. 'Letters to I.I. Shuvalov', in <u>Wiener</u>, I, 242-6.
(Two letters, of 10 and 31 May, 1753).

972. 'Letters to his Patron', in TRL, 618-23.
('On Poets in Garrets', 10 May 1753, 618-20; 'Concerning
Certain Experiments', 31 May 1753, 620-23).

'Pis'mo o pol'ze stekla' (1752)

973. 'Letter on the Use of Glass. To the Chamberlain and Rector
of Moscow University, Ivan Ivanovich Shuvalov, Written in the
Year 1752', in Segel, I, 210-20.

974. 'Epistle on the Usefulness of Glass', in Brown, 108 (Prose
extracts).

'Pis'mo o pravilakh rossiiskogo stikhotvorstva' (1739)

975. 'Letter on the Rules of Russian Versification', translated by
R. SILBAJORIS, in his Russian Versification... (1968),
70-77. (No.284)

'Slovo pokhval'noe... Petru Velikomu' (1755)

976. 'Oration to the Memory of Peter the Great Delivered before
the Academy of Sciences at St. Petersburgh, on the 26 of April
1755, the Anniversary of the Coronation of Empress Elizabeth',
The Bee, or Literary Weekly Intelligencer, XVII(1793), 265-73;
305-14; XVIII(1794), 10-19.
[Translated by Matthew Guthrie; see No. 179].

977. 'Panegyric to the Sovereign Emperor Peter the Great',
translated by R. HINGLEY, in M. RAEFF, Russian Intellectual
History: An Anthology (New York, 1966), 32-48.

'Utrennie razmyshleniia o Bozh'em velichestve' (1751)

978. 'Morning Meditations', in Bowring, II, 10-11.
Reprinted in Wiener, I, 252-3.

979. 'Morning Reflections on the Greatness of God', translated by
C.F. COXWELL, in his Russian Poems (1929), 25-6.

980. 'Morning Meditations on the Majesty of God', translated by
H. SEGEL, in Segel, I, 206-8.
Reprinted in H.B. SEGEL, The Baroque Poem: A Comparative
Survey (New York, 1974), 194-5.

'Vechernee razmyshlenie o Bozhiem velichestve...' (1748)

981. 'Evening Reflections, on the Majesty of God, on Seeing the
Great Northern Lights', in Bowring, I,
A different version, Bowring, II, 12-14.
Reprinted: first version, Tickler's Magazine, III, 5(1 May
1821), 104; second version, in F.R. GRAHAME, The Progress of
Science... (1865), 44-5; and in Wiener, I, 253-4.

982. 'God's Majesty: An Evening Reflection Aroused by the Aurora
Borealis', translated by C.F. COXWELL, in his Russian Poems
(1929), 26-7.

983. 'Evening Meditation on the Majesty of God on the Occasion of the Great Northern Lights', translated by H. SEGEL, in Segel, I, 203-5.
Reprinted in H.B. SEGEL, The Baroque Poem: A Comparative Survey (New York, 1974), 192-3.

984. [LEEDS, W.H.], 'Lomonosov and his Contemporaries', The Foreign Quarterly Review, XXIII(July, 1839), 316-39, 380-410.

985. [TURNER, C.E.], 'Studies in Modern Russian Literature. I. Lomonosoff', The Reader, VII(27 October 1866), 887-8.
(Includes two stanzas, in prose translation, of 'Ode on the Accession of Catherine II').
Reprinted as 'Studies in Russian Literature: I. Lomonosov', Fraser's Magazine, NS XV(1877), 651-8.

986. DIXON, W.H., 'A Peasant Poet', in his Free Russia, II (1870), 11-20.

987. MARCHANT, F.P., 'The Works of M.V. Lomonosov. Vol. IV. Edited and annotated by Academician M.I. Sukhomlinov', Anglo-Russian Literary Society Proceedings, 66(1913), 89-93.

988. MENSHUTKIN, B.N., Russia's Lomonosov: Chemist, Courtier, Physicist, Poet (Princeton, 1952).

989. KUDRYAVTSEV, B.B., The Life and Work of Mikhail Vasilyevich Lomonosov (Moscow, 1954).

990. HUNTINGTON, W.C., 'Michael Lomonosov and Benjamin Franklin: Two Self-Made Men of the Eighteenth Century', RR, XVIII(1959), 294-306.

991. BUCSELA, J., 'The Role of Lomonosov in the Development of Russian Literary Style' (Ph.D., University of Wisconsin, 1963).

992. LANGEVIN, L., 'Lomonosov and the Science of his Day', Impact of Science on Society, XIII(1963), 93-119.

993. JOHNSON, C.A., 'Lomonosov's Dedication to his Russian Grammar', SR, XXIII, 2(1964), 328-32.

994. BUCSELA, J., 'Lomonosov's Literary Debut', SEEJ, XI (1967), 405-22.

995. DVOICHENKO-MARKOV, D.L., 'Lomonosov and the Capture of the Fortress of Khotin in 1739', Balkan Studies, VIII(1967), 65-74.

996. KOGAN, Yu.Yu., 'M.V. Lomonosov and Religion', Cahiers d'Histoire mondiale. Journal of World History. Cuadernos de Historia mundial, X(1967), 519-50.

997. SMITH, M.N., 'Old Russian Literature--Michael Vasilievich Lomonosov (1711-1765)', South Central Bulletin, XXVIII(1968), 126-8.

998. VASETSKY, G., Lomonosov's Philosophy (Moscow, 1968).

999. JONES, D.N., 'M.V. Lomonosov: The Formative Years, 1711-1742' (Ph.D., University of North Carolina, 1969).

1000. JOHNSTON, R., '"An Original Champion of Enlightenment": M.V. Lomonosov and Russian Education in the 18th Century', in Symbolae in Honorem Georgii Y. Shevelov, edited by W.E. HARKINS, O. HORBATSCH and J.P. HURSKY (Munich, 1971), 373-94.

1001. LEICESTER, A.M., 'The Electrical Theories of M.V. Lomonosov', Annals of Science, XXX(1973), 299-319.

1002. TICHOVSKIS, H., 'Lomonosov's View on the Relation between Baltic and Slavic Languages', in Baltic Linguistics and Literatures: Papers from the Third Conference on Baltic Studies, Toronto, May 11-14 1972 (Columbus, 1973), 143-9.

1003. KJETSAA, G., 'Lomonosov's Sound Characteristics', Scando-Slavica, 20(1974), 77-94.

1004. MARTIN, A., 'Lomonosov's Rhetoric' (Ph.D., New York University, 1974).

1005. STACY, R.H., Russian Literary Criticism: A Short History (Syracuse, 1974).
(Pp. 13-24, 'Lomonosov').

1006. HEIM, M., 'Lomonosov's La Fontaine', SEEJ, XX, 3(1976), 224-30.

1007. KJETSAA, G., 'Sound and Meaning according to Lomonosov', in The Computer in Literary and Linguistic Studies. Papers from the Third International Symposium on the Use of the Computer in Linguistic and Literary Research, Cardiff, April, 1974, edited by A. JONES and R.F. CHURCHHOUSE (Cardiff, 1976), 230-39.

1008. GLEASON, W., 'The Course of Russian History according to an Eighteenth Century Layman', Laurentian University Review, X, 1(1977), 17-29 (State and Autocracy in Imperial Russian and Soviet Historiography).

1009. YANCEY, J.V., 'Baroque Elements in the Poetry of M.V. Lomonosov' (Ph.D., University of British Columbia, 1977).

1010. VICKERY, W.N., 'A Comparison of Samples of Lomonosov's and Puškin's Four-Foot Iambs', in American Contributions to the Eighth International Congress of Slavists, I, Linguistics and Poetics, edited by H. BIRNBAUM (Columbus, 1978), 727-56.

1011. VROON, R., 'Velemir Chlebnikov's "Chadži-Tarchan" and the Lomonosovian Tradition', Russian Literature, IX, 1(1981), 107-31.

LOPUKHIN, I.V. (1756-1816)

1012. LIPSKI, A., 'A Russian Mystic Faces the Age of Rationalism
and Revolution: Thought and Activity of Ivan Vladimirovich
Lopukhin', Church History, XXXVI, 2(1967), 1-19.

1013. TORKE, H.J., 'Introduction', in I.V. LOPUKHIN, Zapiski
(Newtonville, 1976), 1-7.

LUKIN, V.I. (1737-94)

1014. McLEAN, H., 'The Adventures of an English Comedy in
Eighteenth-Century Russia: Dodsley's Toy Shop and Lukin's
Ščepetil'nik', in American Contributions to the Fifth
International Congress of Slavists, Sofia, September 1963.
II. Literary Contributions (The Hague, 1963), 201-12.

1015. McCORMICK, P.A., 'The Critical Ideas of Vladimir Lukin'
(Ph.D., Georgetown University, 1973).

L'VOV, N.A. (1751-1803)

'Epistola k A.M. Bakuninu iz Pavlovskogo, iiunia 14, 1797'

1016. 'Epistle to A.M. Bakunin from Pavlovsk, June 14, 1797', in
Brown, 424-5 (Prose extracts).

'Noch' v chukhonskoi izbe na pustyne'

1017. 'Night in a Finnish Hut in the Open Plain', in Brown, 426
(Prose extracts).

'Pesnia' ('Kak, byvalo, ty v temnoi oseni')(1790s)

1018. 'Now, it seems, you, darling, beautiful sun', in Brown, 423
(Prose translation).

'Russkii 1791 god'

1019. 'The Russian Year 1791', in Brown, 418-19 (Prose extracts).

'Solnyshko saditsia' (1790s)

1020. 'The Precious Sun is setting', in Brown, 422 (Prose
translation).

1021. MOSER, C.A., 'The Problem of the Igor Tale', CSS, VII, 2
(1973), 135-54.
(Proposes L'vov as the forger of the Igor Tale).

L'VOV, P.Iu. (1770-1825)

Rossiiskaia Pamela (1789)

1022. 'A Utopian Fragment from The Russian Pamela', translated by
S.L. BAEHR, RLT, 20/21.

MAIKOV, V.I. (1728-78)

Elisei... (1771)

1023. 'The Battle of the Zimogorans and Valdayans', in Wiener, I,
263-7 (Prose extract).

1024. 'Elizei, or Bacchus Enraged: A Poem', translated by H. SEGEL,
in Segel, II, 127-79.

'Kon' znatnoi prirody' (pub.1767)

1025. 'The Horses were Sold', in Brown, 281 (Prose translation).

'Oda o vkuse. Aleksandru Petrovichu Sumarokovu' (1776)

1026. 'Ode on Taste, to Alexander Petrovich Sumarokov', in Brown,
279-80 (Prose translation).

'Povar i portnoi' (1766)

1027. 'The Cook and the Tailor', in Wiener, I, 267-8 (Prose
translation).

'Sonet k Mikhailu Nikitichu Murav'evu' (1775)

1028. 'Sonnet to Murav'ev', in Brown, 441 (Prose translation).

'Voina'(pub.1773)

1029. 'War', in Brown, 278 (Prose translation of six stanzas).

1030. CURTIS, J.M., 'Vasilij Majkov, an Eighteenth-Century Russian
Poet' (Ph.D., Columbia University, 1968).

1031. UNBEGAUN, B.O., 'Metre and Language: Vasilij Majkov's Arkas',
in Slavic Poetics, edited by R. JAKOBSON et alii (The Hague-
Paris, 1973), 477-80.

MURAV'EV, M.N. (1757-1807)

'Boleslav, korol' pol'skii'

1032. 'Boleslav, King of Poland', in Bowring, II, 179-83.

'Epistola k N.R.R***' (1776)

1033. 'Epistle to N.R.R.', in Brown, 445 (Prose extracts).

'K bogine Neve'

1034. 'To the Goddess of the Neva', in Bowring, II, 175-8.
Reprinted, Wiener, I, 395-7.

1035. 'To the Goddess of the Neva', in Brown, 452-3 (Prose
translation).

'K Khemnitseru' (1776)

1036. 'To Khemnitser', in Brown, 447 (Prose extracts).

'Miloe ditia' (17??)

1037. 'The Dear Child', in Brown, 452 (Prose translation).

'Obitatel' predmest'ia'

1038. 'An Inhabitant of a Suburb', translated by C.L. DRAGE, in
RLT, 20/21.

'Oda shestaia. K D***' (1776)

1039. 'Sixth Ode. To D[mitrevsky]', in Brown, 446 (Prose extracts).

'Otryvok' (1780?)

1040. 'Fragment', in Brown, 448 (Prose translation).

'Pis'mo k ***' (1783)

1041. 'Letter to ***', in Brown, 449 (Prose translation).

'Poslanie o legkom stikhotvorstve' (1783)

1042. 'Epistle on Light Verse', in Brown, 451-2 (Prose extracts).

'Romans, s kaledonskogo iazyka perelozhennyi' (1804)

1043. 'Romance, paraphrased from the Caledonian Tongue', in Brown,
454 (Prose translation).

'Roshcha' (1778)

1044. 'The Grove', in Brown, 442-3 (Prose extracts).

'Sonet k muzam' (1775)

1045. 'Sonnet to the Muses', in Brown, 440 (Prose translation).

'Sonet. K Vasiliiu Ivanovichu Maikovu' (1775)

1046. 'Sonnet to Vasily Ivanovich Maikov', in Brown, 440-1 (Prose
translation).

'Vremia' (1775)

1047. 'Time', in Brown, 444-5 (Prose translation).

1048. RADEZKY, I., 'M.N. Murav'ev' (Ph.D., Columbia University,
1980).

NELEDINSKII-MELETSKII, Iu.A. (1752-1828)

'Dni schastlivy minovalis'' (1796)

1049. 'The days of happiness have passed', in <u>Brown</u>, 474 (Prose translation).

'Milaia vechor sidela' (1795)

1050. 'Song' ('Under the oak-tree, near the rill'), in <u>Bowring</u>, I(2nd edition), 185-6.

1051. 'My love was sitting yesterday', in <u>Brown</u>, 474 (Prose translation)

'Stansy'

1052. 'Stanzas', in <u>Lewis</u>, 40-1.
Reprinted in <u>Wiener</u>, I, 394-5.

'Temire' (1782)

1053. 'To Temira', in <u>Brown</u>, 473 (Prose extracts).

'Ty velish' mne ravnodushnym' (1792)

1054. 'You bid me be indifferent', in <u>Brown</u>, 474 (Prose translation).

'Vyidu ia na rechen'ku'

1055. 'Song' ('To the streamlet I'll repair'), in <u>Bowring</u>, I, 187-9.
Reprinted in <u>Wiener</u>, I, 393-4.

O.N.E.

1056. 'Song' ('He whom misery, dark and dreary'), in <u>Bowring</u>, I, 190-1.

NEPLIUEV, I.I. (1693-1773)

1057. LEVENTER, H., 'Introduction to the Memoirs of Ivan I. Nepliuev', in I.I. NEPLIUEV, <u>Zapiski, 1693-1773</u> (Reprint, Cambridge, 1974), i-xi.

NIKITIN, V.N. (1737-1809)

1058. BARRATT, G.R.V., 'Vasily Nikitin: A Note on an Eighteenth-Century Oxonian', <u>Eighteenth-Century Studies</u>, VIII, 1(1974), 75-99.

NIKOLEV, N.P. (1758-1815)

Samoliubivyi stikhotvorets (1775)

1059. 'The Self-Loving Poet', in Brown, 348-9 (Extracts from Acts I and II).

NOVIKOV, N.I. (1744-1818)

'Angliiskaia progulka'

1060. 'The English Promenade', translated by W.G. JONES, in RLT, 20/21.

'O vospitanii i nastavlenii detei' (1783)

1061. 'On the Upbringing and Instruction of Children', translated by V.SNOW, in M. RAEFF, Russian Intellectual History: An Anthology (New York, 1966), 68-86.

Truten' (1770)

1062. 'From "The Drone"', in Wiener, I, 332-5. ('Recipe for His Excellency, Mr Lacksense'; 'The Laughing Democritos').

1063. 'Letter to the Publisher, 6 June 1769', in PRR, 625-7.

1064. 'The Polemics between Catherine and Novikov', translated by H. SEGEL, in Segel, I, 260-300. (Includes Catherine's essays from Vsiakaia vsiachina).

1065. 'Extracts from The Drone', in Brown, 167-71.

Utrennii svet (1777)

1066. 'On Man's High Estate', translated by V. SNOW, in M. RAEFF, Russian Intellectual History: An Anthology (New York, 1966), 62-7.

Zhivopisets (1772-3)

See Nos.464, 1267.

1067. McARTHUR, G.H., 'The Novikov Circle in Moscow, 1779-1792' (Ph.D., Rochester University, 1968).

1068. McARTHUR, G.H., 'Catherine II and the Masonic Circle of N.I. Novikov', CSS, IV(1970), 529-46.

1069. JONES, W.G., 'The Closure of Novikov's Truten'', SEER, L, 118(1972), 107-11.

1070. JONES, W.G., 'Novikov's Naturalized Spectator', in Garrard, 149-65.

1071. JONES, W.G., 'The Year of Novikov's Birth', <u>SGECRN</u>, 2 (1974), 30-2.

1072. WEINBAUM, A., 'N.I. Novikov (1744-1818): An Interpretation of his Career and Ideas' (Ph.D., Columbia University, 1975).

1073. VON HERZEN, M.A., 'Nikolai Ivanovich Novikov: The St. Petersburg Years' (Ph.D., University of California at Berkeley, 1975).

1074. SERMAN, I.Z., 'Novikov and <u>The Tatler</u>', translated by G.S. SMITH, <u>SGECRN</u>, 5(1977), 37-8.

1075. JONES, W.G., 'The <u>Morning Light</u> Charity Schools, 1777-80', <u>SEER</u>, LXVI, 1(1978), 47-67.

1076. OKENFUSS, M.J., 'The Novikov Problem: An English Perspective', in <u>GBR</u>, 97-108.

1077. McARTHUR, G.H., 'Freemasonry and Enlightenment in Russia: The Views of N.I. Novikov', <u>CSS</u>, XIV, 3(1980), 361-75.

PELSKII, P.A. (1765-1803)

'Plach muzha'

1078. 'The Husband's Lament', in <u>Lewis</u>, 37-8.

PETROV, V.P. (1736-99)

'Oda na pobedy v Moree'

1079. 'On the Victory of the Russian over the Turkish Fleet', in <u>Bowring</u>, II, 191-204.
Reprinted in <u>Wiener</u>, I, 291-8.

'Smert' moego syna marta 1795 goda'

1080. 'My Son's Death, March, 1793', in <u>Brown</u>, 275 (Prose extract).

1081. MARTYNOV, I.F., 'Notes on V.P. Petrov and his Stay in England (New Materials)', <u>SGECRN</u>, 7(1979), 29-31.

PLATON, Metropolitan (1737-1812)

1082. Καrnκnἰιs - The Great Catechism of the Holy Catholic <u>Apostolic and Orthodox Church</u>, translated from the Greek by J.T.S. (1867).

Pravoslavnoe uchenie, ili sokrashchennaia khristianskaia bogosloviia (1765).

1083. The Present State of the Greek Church in Russia; or, a Summary of Christian Divinity, translated from the Slavonian. With a preliminary memoir on the ecclesiastical establishment in Russia, by R. PINKERTON (Edinburgh, 1814; New York, 1815).

'Rech' E.I.V.G.I. Aleksandru Pavlovichu po sovershenii koronovaniia 1801 goda sent. 15'

1084. 'The Oration of Plato, Archbishop of Mosco, on crowning Alexander the First, 15th of Sept. 1801', The London Chronicle, XCI, 66880(1802), 49.
        [Translated by M. GUTHRIE].

'Slovo pri sluchae sovershaemykh molitv nad grobom Petra Velikogo' (1770).

1085. An Oration Preached by Order of Her Imperial Majesty, on the Tomb of Peter the Great, in the Cathedral Church of St. Petersburg (1770).
        [Translated by J. HINCHCLIFFE from the French version].

O.N.E.

1086. The Orthodox Doctrine of the Apostolic Eastern Church; or, A Compendium of Christian Theology, translated from the Greek... to which is appended a Treatise on Melchisedec (1857).

1087. ANON., Review of An Oration... (No. 1085), Monthly Review, XLV(1770), 414.

PNIN, I.P. (1773-1805)

1088. RAMER, S.C., 'Ivan Pnin and Vasily Popugaev: A Study in Russian Political Thought' (Ph.D., Columbia University, 1971).

1089. CROSS, A.G., 'Pnin and the Sankt-Peterburgskii zhurnal (1798)', CSS, VII, 1(1973), 78-84.

1090. RAMER, S.C., 'The Traditional and the Modern in the Writings of Ivan Pnin', SR, XXXV, 3(1975), 539-59.

POPOV, M.I. (1742-90)

'Pesnia'
1091. 'In parting from me', in Brown, 197.

POPOVSKII, N.N. (1730-60)

'Oda... Elizavete Petrovne' (1754)

1092. 'Ode to Elizaveta Petrovna', in Brown, 269 (Two stanzas).

POROSHIN, S.A. (1741-69)

Zapiski

1093. 'From his "Diary"', in Wiener, I, 321-6.

POSOSHKOV, I.T. (1652-1726)

Kniga o skudosti i bogatstve (1725)

1094. 'The Book on Poverty and Wealth', in Wiener, I, 205-10.
(Excerpts from the chapters 'On Merchants' and 'On the
Peasantry').

1095. O'BRIEN, B., 'Ivan Pososhkov: Russian Critic of Mercantilist
Principles', SR, XIV, 4(1955), 503-11.

1096. PAPMEHL, K., 'Pososhkov as Thinker', Études slaves et est-
européennes, VI(1961), 80-7.

1097. LEWITTER, L.R., 'Ivan Tikhomirovich Pososhkov (1652-1726) and
"The Spirit of Capitalism"', SEER, LI, 125(1973), 524-53.

PROKOPOVICH, FEOFAN (1681-1736)

Dukhovnyi reglament (1721)

1098. 'A Regulation Spiritual', translated by T. CONSETT, in his
The Present State and Regulations of the Church of Russia,
I (1729), 1-202.

1099. 'From "The Spiritual Reglement"', in Wiener, I, 212-14.

'Feofan arkhiepiskop Novgorodskii k avtoru satiry' (1730)

1100. 'To the Author of the Satire "To My Mind"', translated by
H. SEGEL, in Segel, I, 164.

1101. 'To the Composer of the Satire', in Brown, 33.

'O smerti Petra Velikogo. Kratkaia povest'' (1727)

1102. 'A Brief Relation of the Death of Peter the Great',
translated by T. CONSETT, in his The Present State and
Regulations of the Church of Russia, II (1729), 254-78.

Pervoe uchenie otrokom

1103. The Russian Catechism, Compos'd and Publish'd by Order of the Czar, translated by J.T. Philipps (1723, 2nd ed. 1725). (Translated from the German).

'Plachet pastushok v dolgom nenast'e' (1730)

1104. 'The Shepherd Mourns in the Long-lasting Bad Weather', in Brown, 23-4.

Slovo na pogrebenie... Ekateriny Alekseevnoi (1727)

1105. 'An Oration on the Death of... Catharina Alexievna', translated by T. CONSETT, in his The Present State and Regulations of the Church of Russia, II (1729), 431-40.

'Slovo na pogrebenie... Petra Velikogo' (1725)

1106. 'An Oration at the Funeral of... Peter the Great', translated by T. CONSETT, in his The Present State and Regulations of the Church of Russia, II (1729), 279-87.

1107. 'Funeral Sermon on Peter the Great', in Wiener, I, 214-18.

'Slovo o vlasti i chesti tsarskoi' (1718)

1108. 'Sermon on Royal Authority and Honor', translated by H.G. LUNT, in M. RAEFF, Russian Intellectual History: An Anthology (New York, 1966), 14-30.

1109. ŠERECH, J., 'On Teofan Prokopovic as Writer and Preacher in his Kiev Period', HSS, II(1954), 211-24.

1110. GRAHAM, H., 'Theophan Prokopovich and the Ecclesiastical Ordinance', Church History, XXV(1956), 127-35.

1111. CASSELTON, A.F., 'Christian Enlightenment in Feofan Prokopovich's Tragicomedy "Vladimir"' (M.A., University of Auckland, 1967).

1112. DELLA CAVA, O.T., 'Sermons of Feofan Prokopovič: Themes and Style' (Ph.D., Columbia University, 1972).

1113. CRACRAFT, J., 'Feofan Prokopovich', in Garrard, 75-105.

1114. CRACRAFT, J., 'Feofan Prokopovich: A Bibliography of his Works', OSP, NS VIII(1975), 1-36.

1115. CRACRAFT, J., 'Prokopovič's Kiev Period Reconsidered', Harvard Ukrainian Studies, II(1978), 138-57.

1116. CRACRAFT, J., 'Did Feofan Prokopovich Really Write Pravda Voli Monarshei?', SR, XL, 2(1981), 173-93.

'Dnevnik odnoi nedeli' (?)

1117. 'Diary of a Week', in Brown, 551-2 (Extracts).

1118. 'Diary of One Week', translated by T. PAGE, in RLT, 20/21.

'O cheloveke, o ego smertnosti i bessmertii' (1792)

1119. 'On Man, his Mortality and Immortality', translated by F.Y. GLADNEY and G.L. KLINE, in Russian Philosophy, I, edited by J.M. EDIE, J.P. SCANLAN and M.-B. ZELDIN (Chicago, 1965), 77-100.

'Osmnadtsatoe stoletie' (pub. 1807)

1120. 'The Eighteenth Century', translated by H. SEGEL, in Segel, II, 438-40.

Puteshestvie iz Peterburga v Moskvu (1790)

1121. A Journey from St. Petersburg to Moscow, translated by L.WIENER, edited with an Introduction and Notes by R.P. THALER (Cambridge, Mass., 1958).
(Earlier versions of four chapters appeared in Wiener, I, 362-70: 'Departure', 'Sofiya', 'Tosna', 'Lyubani').
Extracts reprinted in Segel, I, 357-92.

'Sapficheskie strofy' (1801)

1122. 'Sapphic Stanzas', translated by V.de S. PINTO, in C.M. BOWRA, A Second Book of Russian Verse (1948), 4.

1123. 'Sapphic Strophes', in Brown, 492.

'Ty khochesh' znat', kto ia? chto ia? kuda ia edu?' (1791)

1124. 'You want to know who I am?', in Brown, 487.

'Vol'nost'' (1781-3)

1125. 'Liberty', in Brown, 485-7 (Prose extracts).

'Zhuravli' (1797-1801)

1126. 'Cranes', in Brown, 490 (Prose translation).

1127. EVGENIEV, B., Alexander Radishchev. A Russian Humanist of the 18th Century (1946).

1128. HECHT, D., 'Alexander Radishchev: Pioneer Russian Abolitionist', American Review on the Soviet Union, VII, 4 (1946), 45-50.

1129. LANG, D.M., 'Radishchev and Sterne. An Episode in Russian Sentimentalism', Revue de littérature comparée, XXI(1947), 254-60.

1130. LANG, D.M., 'Radishchev and the Legislative Commission of Alexander I', <u>SR</u>, VI, 2(1947), 11-24.

1131. LANG, D.M., 'Some Western Sources of Radishchev's Thought', <u>Revue des Etudes Slaves</u>, XXV(1949), 73-86.

1132. LANG, D.M., 'Alexander Nikolaevich Radishchev and his Contacts with French and German Thinkers' (Ph.D., Cambridge University, 1950).

1133. LASERSON, M.M., 'Alexander Radishchev--An Early Admirer of America', <u>RR</u>, IX(1950), 179-86.

1134. BECK, L.N., 'Pennsylvania and an Early Russian Radical', <u>Pennsylvania Magazine of History and Biography</u>, LXXV(1951), 193-6.

1135. THALER, R.P., 'The French Tutor in Radishchev and Pushkin', <u>RR</u>, XIII(1954), 210-12.

1136. THALER, R.P., 'Catherine II's Reaction to Radishchev', <u>Études slaves et est-européennes</u>, II(1957), 154-60.

1137. THALER, R.P., 'Radishchev, Britain, and America', <u>HSS</u>, IV (1957), 59-75.

1138. McCONNELL, A., 'Radishchev's Political Thought', <u>SR</u>, IV(1958), 439-53.

1139. THALER, R.P., 'Introduction', in A.N. RADISHCHEV, <u>A Journey from St. Petersburg to Moscow</u> (Cambridge, Mass., 1958), 1-37. (No. 1121).

1140. LANG, D.M., <u>The First Russian Radical. Alexander Radishchev 1749-1802</u> (1959).

1141. McCONNELL, A., 'Pushkin's Literary Gamble', <u>SR</u>, VI(1960), 577-93.

1142. CLARDY, J., 'Radishchev's Notes on the Geography of Siberia', <u>RR</u>, XXI(1962), 362-9.

1143. LANG, D.M., 'Radishchev and Catherine II: New Gleanings from Old Archives', in <u>Essays in Russian and Soviet History in Honor of Geroid Tanquary Robinson</u>, edited by J.S. CURTISS (Leiden, 1963), 20-33.

1144. McCONNELL, A., 'Soviet Images of Radishchev's <u>Journey from St. Petersburg to Moscow</u>, <u>SEEJ</u>, VII(1963), 9-17.

1145. McGREW, R., 'The Russian Intelligentsia from Radishchev to Pasternak', <u>Antioch Review</u>, XXIII(1963), 425-37.

1146. CLARDY, J., <u>The Philosophical Ideas of Alexander Radishchev</u> (New York, 1964).

1147. KOCHAN, L., 'Alexander Radishchev, the First of the Repentant Nobles', HT, XIV, 7(1964), 489-96.

1148. McCONNELL, A., 'Rousseau and Radishchev', SEEJ, VIII(1964), 253-72.

1149. McCONNELL, A., 'Abbé Raynal and a Russian Philosophe', Jahrbücher für Geschichte Osteuropas, XII(1964), 499-512.

1150. McCONNELL, A., A Russian Philosophe: Alexander Radishchev 1749-1802 (The Hague, 1964).

1151. BARRATT, G.R., 'A Note on Radiščev and Pugačovščina', Etudes slaves et est-europeennees, XVIII(1973), 66-78.

1152. PAGE, T., 'The Spiritual Conflict of A.N. Radiščev (1749-1802)' (Ph.D., Columbia University, 1973).

1153. HARVIE, J.A., 'A Russian View of Immortality', Religious Studies, X(1974), 479-85.

1154. SMITH, G.S., 'Radishchev: A Concise Bibliography of Works Published Outside the Soviet Union', SGECRN, 2(1974), 53-61.

1155. PAGE, T., 'Radishchev's Polemic against Sentimentalism in the Cause of Eighteenth-Century Utilitarianism', in Cross, 141-72.

1156. PAGE, T., 'A Radiščev Monstrology: the Journey from Petersburg to Moscow and Later Writings in the Light of French Sources', in American Contributions to the Eighth International Congress of Slavists, II. Literature (Columbus, 1978), 605-29.

1157. MAKOGONENKO, G.P., 'Radishchev and Sterne', translated by G.S. SMITH, in GBR, 84-93.

1158. CROSS, A.G., 'The Black Hole of Calcutta: Radishchev and Frederick Chamier', SGECRN, 8(1980), 52-7.

1159. SHIRAKURA, K., 'On Alexander Radishchev's Ethical Ideas', Japanese Slavic and East European Studies, 2(1981), 57-67.

1160. PAGE, T., 'The "Diary of One Week": Radishchev's Record of Suicidal Despair', in RLT, 20/21.

RZHEVSKII, A.A. (1737-1804)

'Elegiia' ('Muchitel'naia strast'! prestan' menia terzat'') (1763)

1161. 'Turturous passion! Cease to torment me', in Brown, 295-7.

'Elegiia' ('Ne znaiu, otchego ves' dukh moi unyvaet') (1763)

1162. 'I don't know why my whole spirit is despondent', in <u>Brown</u>, 297-8.

'Elegiia' ('Ty zapreshchaesh' mne sebe, moi svet, liubit'') (1763)

1163. 'You forbid me, my light, to love you', in <u>Brown</u>, 297.

'Idilliia' ('Na bregakh tekushchikh rek') (pub.1762)

1164. 'Upon the banks of flowing rivers', in <u>Brown</u>, 298.

'Sonet' ('Gde smertnym obresti na svete sem blazhenstvo?')(pub.1761)

1165. 'Where are mortals to find happiness in this world?', in <u>Brown</u>, 299.

'Stans' ('Potshchimsia my snosit' napasti terpelivo')(pub.1759)

1166. 'Stanzas on Mutability', in <u>Brown</u>, 299-300.

RUBAN, V.G. (1742-95)

<u>Vasil'ia Rubana Nadpisi k kamniiu, ... v podnozhii... litsepodobiia</u>
<u>... Petra Velikogo...</u> (1791)

1167. W..., 'Inscription by Basili Ruban on the Rock which, serves a Pedestal for PETER the first...', in <u>Vasil'ia Rubana</u> <u>k kamniu...</u> (St. Petersburg, 1791). (See No.1168).

1168. CROSS, A.G., 'An English Version (1791) of a Poem by Vasilii Ruban', <u>SGECRN</u>, 7(1979), 38-40. (See No.1167).

SAMBORSKII, A.A. (1732-1815)

1169. CROSS, A.G., 'The Svodnyi katalog: <u>Addenda</u> and <u>Corrigenda</u> from British Sources', <u>SGECRN</u>, 9(1981), 51-6.

SHAFIROV, P.P. (1669-1739)

<u>Rassuzhdenie kakie zakonnye prichiny...</u> (1717)

1170. 'A Discourse Concerning the Causes of the War between Russia and Sweden', in F.C. WEBER , <u>The Present State of Russia</u>, II (1722), 237-351.
Facsimile reprint, 1968.
Reprint: P.P. SHAFIROV, <u>A Discourse concerning the Just</u> <u>Causes of the War between Sweden and Russia: 1700-1721</u> (Dobbs Ferry, 1973).

1171. BUTLER, W.E., 'Shafirov: Diplomatist of Petrine Russia', HT, XXIII, 10(1973), 699-704.

1172. BUTLER, W.E., 'P.P. Shafirov and the Law of Nations', in P.P. SHAFIROV, A Discourse concerning the Just War... (Dobbs Ferry, 1973), 1-39 (No. 1170).

SHAKHOVSKOI, Ia.P. (1705-77)

1173. JONES, R.E., 'Introduction', in Ia.P. SHAKHOVSKOI, Zapiski, 1709-1777 (Cambridge, 1974), i-iv.

SHCHERBATOV, M.M. (1733-90)

O povrezhdenii nravov v Rossii (pub.1858)

1174. 'On the Corruption of Morals in Russia', in Wiener, I, 287-91 (Extracts).

1175. On the Corruption of Morals in Russia, translated by A. LENTIN (Cambridge, 1969).

'Proshenie Moskvy o zabvenii ee' (1787, pub. 1860)

1176. 'Petition of the City of Moscow on Being Relegated to Oblivion', translated by V. SNOW, in M. RAEFF, Russian Intellectual History: An Anthology (New York, 1966), 50-5.

'Primernoe vremiaischislitel'noe polozhenie...' (?, pub. 1890)

1177. 'The Pace of Russia's Modernization', translated by V. SNOW, in M. RAEFF, Russian Intellectual History: An Anthology (New York, 1966), 56-60.

1178. RAEFF, M., 'State and Nobility in the Ideology of M.M. Shcherbatov', SR, XIX(1960), 363-79.

1179. AFFERICA, J.M., 'The Political and Social Thought of M.M. Shcherbatov (1733-1790)' (Ph.D., Harvard University, 1967).

1180. LENTIN, A., 'M.M. Shcherbatov, with Special Reference to his Memoir 'On the Corruption of Morals in Russia'' (Ph.D., Cambridge, 1969).

1181. LENTIN, A., 'Introduction', in M.M. SHCHERBATOV, On the Corruption of Morals in Russia (Cambridge, 1969), 1-102.

1182. LENTIN, A., 'Beccaria, Shcherbatov, and the Question of Capital Punishment in Eighteenth-Century Russia', CSP, XXIV (1982), 128-37.

SHISHKOV, A.S. (1754-1841)

O.N.E.

1183. 'Poor People', translated by C.F. COXWELL, in his Russian
       Poems (1929), 36-7.

SKOVORODA, G.S. (1722-94)

'Razgovor piati putnikov o istinnom shchastii v zhizni'

1184. 'A Conversation among Five Travelers Concerning Life's True
       Happiness', translated by G.L. KLINE, in Russian Philosophy,
       I, edited by J.M. EDIE, J.P. SCANLAN and M.-B. ZELDIN
       (Chicago, 1965), 26-57.

'Sokrat v Rossii'

1185. 'Socrates in Russia', translated by G.L. KLINE, in Russian
       Philosophy, I, edited by J.M. EDIE, J.P. SCANLAN and M.-B.
       ZELDIN (Chicago, 1965), 17-18.

'Zhizn' Grigoriia Skovorody'

1186. 'The Life of Grigory Skovoroda', translated by G.L. KLINE, in
       Russian Philosophy, I, edited by J.M. EDIE, J.P.SCANLAN and
       M.-B. ZELDIN (Chicago, 1965), 19-25.

(Letters, written in Latin)

1187. 'Four Letters to Mikhail Kovalinskii', translated by J.M.
       EDIE, in Russian Philosophy, I, edited by J.M. EDIE, J.P.
       SCANLAN and M.-B. ZELDIN (Chicago, 1965), 58-62.

1188. SCHERER, S.P., 'The Life and Thought of Russia's First Lay
       Theologian, Grigorij Savvic Skovoroda (1722-1794)' (Ph.D.,
       Ohio State University, 1969).

1189. FUHRMANN, J.T., 'The First Russian Philosopher's Search for
       the Kingdom of God', in Essays in Russian Intellectual
       History, edited by L.B. BLAIR (Austin and London, 1971),
       33-72.

SUMAROKOV, A.P. (1718-77)

1190. Selected Tragedies of A.P. Sumarokov, translated by R. and R.
       FORTUNE (Evanston, 1970). Contains 'Khorev, a Tragedy',
       'Hamlet, a Tragedy', and 'Semira, a Tragedy'.

'Beznogii soldat'

1191. 'The Legless Soldier', in Brown, 142 (Prose translation).

'Chetyre otveta'

1192. 'Four Answers', in Wiener, I, 261-2.

Dve epistoly (1748)

1193. 'Two Epistles', in Segel, I, 224-38.

Dmitrii samozvanets (1771)

1194. Demetrius, the Impostor; a tragedy by Alexander Soumarokove [translated by A.G. EVSTAV'EV] (1806).

1195. 'The False Demetrius', in Wiener, I, 255-7. (Act II, scenes 1 and 7).

1196. 'Dimitrii the Impostor', translated by R. and R. FORTUNE, in Segel, II, 396-434. Reprinted in No. 1190, 189-229.

'Elegiia' ('Stradai, priskorbnyi dukh!') (1768)

1197. 'Elegy', in Brown, 133-4 (Prose translation).

'Ekloga. Enona'

1198. 'Enona, an Eclogue', in H. STORCH, The Picture of Petersburg (1801), 385-7. (No. 51; translated from German by W. TOOKE).

'Epistola o stikhotvorstve'

1199. 'The thund'ring ode, resounding in the ear', in H. STORCH, The Picture of Petersburg (1801), 388. (No. 51; translated from German by W. TOOKE).

Gamlet: See No.1190.

'K g. Dmitrevskomu na smert' F.G. Volkova'

1200. 'Melpomene, unite thy tears with mine', in W. COXE, Travels into Poland..., II(1784), 203. (No. 43; translated by W. COXE from the French prose paraphrase by N.G. Leclerc).

Khorev: See No.1190.

'Khor ko prevratnomu svetu' (1763, pub. 1781)

1201. 'Chorus to a Topsy-Turvey World', translated by W.E. HARKINS, in Segel, I, 244-6.

'Kto khulit franmazonov'

1202. 'He who finds fault with Free Masons', in Brown, 162.

'Nastavlenie synu' (1774)

1203. 'Instruction to a Son', in Wiener, I, 257-60.

1204. 'Instruction to a Son', in Segel, I, 249-51.

'Nedostatok vremeni' (pub.1781)

1205. 'Lack of Time', in Brown, 141-2 (Prose translation).

'Oda vzdornaia I' (pub.1759)

1206. 'First Nonsense Ode', in Brown, 99 (Prose translation).

'Oda vzdornaia II'(pub.1759)

1207. 'Second Nonsense Ode', in Brown, 99-100 (Prose translation).

'Oda... Ekaterine... na den' rozhdeniia... 1768'

1208. 'Ode to the Sovereign Catherine II on the Day of her Birth, April 21, 1768', in Brown, 117 (Prose translation of three stanzas).

'Oda... Pavlu Pervomu v den' ego tezoimenitstva' (1771)

1209. 'Ode to the Sovereign Prince Paul Petrovich on his Name Day', in Brown, 117 (Prose translation of four stanzas).

Opekun (1764-5)

1210. 'The Guardian', in Brown, 129 (Three speeches).

'Otvet na odu Vasil'iu Ivanovichu Maikovu'(pub.1776)

1211. 'Reply to the Ode of Vasily Ivanovich Maikov', in Brown, 280 (Prose translation).

'O velichii Bozhiem'

1212. 'Ode on the Infinite Greatness of the Deity', in H. STORCH, The Picture of Petersburg (1801), 387-8.
(No. 51; translated from German by W. TOOKE).

'Pesnia' ('Ne grusti, moi svet! Mne grustno i samoi...')(pub.1770)

1213. 'Song' ('Do not grieve, my love, I grieve enough for two'), translated by W.E. HARKINS, in Segel, I, 248.

'Pesnia' ('Tshchetno ia skryvaiu serdtsa skorbi liuty')(pub.1759)

1214. 'A Song', translated by C.F. COXWELL, in his Russian Poems (1929), 28.

'Porcha iazyka' (1769)

1215. 'To the Corrupters of Language', in Wiener, I, 260 (Prose translation).

'Pir u l'va'(pub.1762)

1216. 'A Fable: A Feast at the Lion's', translated by B. COHEN, in Segel, I, 240-1.

1217. 'At the Lion's House: A Fable', in B. RAFFEL, Russian Poetry under the Tsars (Albany, 1971), 16-17.

'Posel osel'(pub.1781)
1218. 'The Ass as Ambassador', in Brown, 141.

Rogonosets po voobrazheniiu (1772)
1219. 'Imaginary Cuckold', in Brown, 130-1 (Translation of dialogues from Act I, scene 13).

'Satira: O chestnosti'(pub.1774)
1220. 'Satire: On Nobility', in Brown, 135.

Semira: See No. 1190.

'Shalun'ia'(pub.1781)
1221. 'The Empty-Headed Girl', in Brown, 141 (Prose translation).

'Usluzhlivyi komar'
1222. 'The Helpful Gnat', in Wiener, I, 260-1 (Prose translation).

'Uzhe voskhodit solntse' (1755)
1223. 'Already the sun is rising...', in Brown, 144.

'Voina orlov' (c. 1762)
1224. 'The War of the Eagles', in Brown, 140 (Prose translation).

'Zhuki i pchely' (1752)
1225. 'Beetles and Bees', in Brown, 139-40 (Prose translation).

'Zmeia i pila'(pub.1762)
1226. 'The Snake and the Saw', in Brown, 140 (Prose translation).

1227. ANON., Review of Demetrius, the Impostor... (No. 1194), Gentleman's Magazine, LXXVI, part 2(1806), 747.

1228. ANON., Review of Demetrius, the Impostor... (No. 1194), Annual Review..., V(1807), 537-8.

1229. ANON., Review of Demetrius, the Impostor... (No. 1194), Literary Journal, II(September, 1806), 334.

1230. TURNER, C.E., 'Studies in Russian Literature. IV. Sumarokoff', Fraser's Magazine, NS XV(1877), 694-700.

1231. LANG, D.M., 'Boileau and Sumarokov. The Manifesto of Russian Classicism', MLR, XLIII(1948), 500-6.

1232. LANG, D.M., 'Sumarokov's "Hamlet". A Misjudged Russian Tragedy of the 18th Century', MLR, XLIII(1948), 67-72.

1233. LANG, D.M., 'A Russian Dramatist's Views on Corneille and Voltaire', Revue de litterature comparée, 1(1949), 86-92.

1234. FIZER, J., 'Introduction', in <u>Selected Tragedies of A.P.</u>
      <u>Sumarokov</u> (Evanston, 1970), 3-39 (No. 1190).

1235. GLEASON, W., 'Sumarokov's Political Ideals: A Reappraisal of
      his Role as a Critic of Catherine II's Policies', <u>CSS</u>, XVIII,
      4(1976), 415-26.

1236. GREEN, M., '<u>Boris Godunov</u>: A Classical Tragedy in Disguise?'
      <u>SGECRN</u>, 6(1978), 36-40.

1237. TOOMRE, J.S., 'Sumarokov's Adaptation of <u>Hamlet</u> and the "To
      Be or Not to Be" Soliloquy', <u>SGECRN</u>, 9(1981), 6-20.

TATISHCHEV, V.N. (1686-1750)

'Dukhovnaia'

1238. <u>The Testament of B. Tatischef</u>, translated from the Russian
      manuscript by J. Martinof (Paris, 1860).

<u>Istoriia Rossiiskaia s samykh drevneishikh vremen...</u>

1239. 'From "The Russian History"', in <u>Wiener</u>, I, 219-23.

'Proizvol'noe i soglasnoe rassuzhdenie i mnenie sobravshegosia
shliakhetstva ruskogo o pravlenii gosudarstvennom' (c.1730)

1240. 'The Voluntary and Agreed Dissertation of the Assembled
      Russian Nobility about the State Government', in <u>Dukes</u>,
      I, 20-7.

1241. KOUTAISOFF, E., and A.S.C. ROSS, 'Tatishchev's "Joachim
      Chronicle"', <u>University of Birmingham Historical Journal</u>,
      III(1951-2), 52-63.

1242. KAPLAN, F.I., 'Tatiščev and Kantemir: Two Eighteenth Century
      Exponents of a Russian Bureaucratic Style of Thought',
      <u>Jahrbücher für Geschichte Osteuropas</u>, XIII(1965), 497-510.

1243. DANIELS, R.L., 'V.N. Tatishchev and the Succession Crisis of
      1730', <u>SEER</u>, XLIX, 117(1971), 550-9.

1244. DANIELS, R.L., 'V.N. Tatishchev: Rationalist Historian and
      Theorist of the Petrine Service Nobility' (Ph.D.,
      University of Pennsylvania, 1971).

1245. FEINSTEIN, S.C., 'V.N. Tatishchev and the Development of the
      Concept of State Service in Petrine Russia and Post-Petrine
      Russia' (Ph.D., New York University, 1971).

1246. DANIELS, R., <u>V.N. Tatishchev, Guardian of the Petrine</u>
      <u>Revolution</u> (Philadelphia, 1973).

1247. ZNAYENKO, M.T., 'Tatiščev's Treatment of Slavic Mythology'
      (Ph.D., Columbia University, 1973).

1248. ZNAYENKO, M.T., Gods of the Ancient Slavs: Tatishchev and the Beginnings of Slavic Mythology (Columbus, 1981).

TREDIAKOVSKII, V.K. (1703-69)

'Feoptiia' (1750-4)

1249. 'Theoptia', in Brown, 67-8 (Extracts).

Novyi i kratkii sposob... (1735)

1250. 'A New and Brief Method for Composing Russian Verse', translated by R. SILBAJORIS, in his Russian Versification... (1968), 37-67 (No. 284).

'Novyi i kratkii sposob... (1752)

1251. 'A Method for the Composition of Russian Verse', translated by R. SILBAJORIS, in his Russian Versification... (1968), 101-27.

'Oda o sdache... goroda Gdanska' (1734)

1252. 'Ode on the Surrender of Danzig', in Wiener, I, 230-3 (Prose translation).

1253. 'Solemn Ode on the Surrender of the City of Danzig, July, 1734', in Segel, I, 173-7.

'Pesn' na koronovanie... Anny Ioannovny...' (1730)

1254. 'Song Composed in Hamburg on the Festal Celebration of the Coronation of Her Soveriegn Majesty the Empress Anna Ioannovna... 1730', in Segel, I, 170-1.

'Stikhi pokhval'nye Rossii' (1730)

1255. 'Panegyric Verses to Russia', in Segel, I, 166-7.

1256. RICE, J.L., 'Trediakovsky and the Russian Poetic Genres 1730-1760: Studies in the History of Eighteenth Century Russian Literature' (Ph.D., University of Chicago, 1965).

1257. SERMAN, I.Z., 'Trediakovskii and his Deidamiia: An Unpublished Document', translated by G.S. SMITH, SGECRN, 7(1979), 23-8.

1258. ROSENBERG, K., 'Between Ancients and Moderns: V.K.Trediakovsky and the Theory of Language and Literature' (Ph.D., Yale University, 1980).

1259. ANDERSEN, Z.B., 'The Concept of "Lyric Disorder"', Scando-Slavica, XXVI(1980), 5-18.
(On Trediakovskii and Boileau).

1260. ROSENBERG, V.K., 'Trediakovskii on Sumarokov: the Critical Issues', in RLT, 20/21.

TRETIAKOV, I.A. (174?-76)

1261. TAYLOR, N.W., 'Adam Smith's First Russian Disciple', SEER,
      XLV, 105(1967), 424-38.

VEREVKIN, M.I. (1733-95)

'Zhizn' pokoinogo Mikhaila Vasil'evicha Lomonosova' (1784)

1263. 'Life of Lomonossove, the Celebrated Poet of Russia', The
      Literary Panorama, I(1807), 149-56.
      [Translated by A.G. EVSTAV'EV].

VINOGRADOV, Iu.Iu. (?-1800 or 1801)

'Oda, podnesennaia e.i.v. Ekaterine Velikoi...' (1785)

1264. Ode to Her Imperial Majesty Catherine the Great, Presented
      by the Chief National School at St. Petersburgh, on the Day
      of Her Most Gracious Visit, January the 21st 1785, translated
      by S. WESTON (1815).
      Reprinted in S. WESTON, The Englishman Abroad, Part II:
      Russia, Germany, Italy, France, Spain and Portugal: With
      Specimens, and a Head and Tail-Piece (1824), 1-25.

VINSKY, G.S. (1752-?)

1265. MADARIAGA, I.DE, 'The Memoirs of G.S. Vinsky', in G.S. VINSKY,
      Moe vremia, Zapiski (Cambridge, 1974), i-xvii.

INDEXES

CONTENTS OF MAJOR COLLECTIONS

Segel II: 490, 545, 547, 569-70, 574, 584, 587, 593, 597, 601, 604, 607, 611, 689, 696, 762, 807, 892, 894, 896-7, 900, 903, 906, 908, 910-12, 916, 923, 939, 1024, 1120, 1196

TRL 567, 579, 653, 681, 952, 972

Wiener 441, 489, 507, 509 (reprint), 510, 555, 565 (reprint), 573, 576 (reprint), 595 (reprint), 609 (reprint), 650, 656, 675 (reprint), 677 (reprint), 685, 688, 697, 699, 702, 719, 723, 741, 744 (reprint), 747, 761, 777, 784, 785 (reprint), 816, 898, 922, 936, 940, 946, 965 (reprint), 971, 978 (reprint), 981 (reprint), 1023, 1027, 1034 (reprint), 1052 (reprint), 1055 (reprint), 1062, 1079 (reprint), 1093-4, 1099, 1107, 1121, 1174, 1192, 1195, 1203, 1215, 1222, 1239, 1252, 1266

1753	40			1882	67
1768	41			1887	27
1770	42	1781	43	1890	68
1784	44-5			1895	69
1792	46			1897	70, 711
1794	47, 511			1900	71, 329
1795	512			1902	28-9
1799	513-14			1903	330
1800	48-50, 144, 515, 622, 831			1905	72
1801	51, 328			1907	271
1802	830			1908	73
1803	52, 832			1912	30
1804	53, 833-7			1913	517, 987
1806	1227, 1229			1916	331
1807	1228			1917	842
1816	84			1918	31, 370
1821	25			1921	74
1822	54			1923	160
1824	55			1925	332, 408
1825	838			1927	75
1827	56			1929	32
1829	57			1930	222
1833	58			1931	223
1839	59-60, 269, 984			1932	518
1842	61, 270			1933	333
1846	62-3			1934	161
1848	64			1935	162, 1268
1849	26			1936	210, 224, 334
1850	65			1937	163
1865	66			1938	249
1866	516, 731, 985			1939	519, 712
1870	986			1940	335
1877	516 (reprint), 621, 710, 731-2, 840-1, 985, 1230			1942	336, 949

1943	33
1946	1127-8
1947	34, 232, 1129-30
1948	35, 107, 1231-2
1949	36, 211, 316, 1131, 1233
1950	233-4, 241, 337-8, 1132-3
1951	21, 164, 339, 409, 720, 1134, 1241
1952	250-1, 340, 926, 988
1953	108-9, 341, 410, 890
1954	165-6, 272, 342, 989, 1109, 1135
1955	167, 235, 273, 343, 411-12, 558, 942, 1095
1956	15 (continuing), 76, 145, 252, 274, 344, 500, 732, 1110
1957	110, 371, 413, 733, 843-4, 962, 1136-7
1958	168-9, 253-4, 345-6, 734, 845, 957, 1138-9
1959	275-6, 347, 414, 846, 950, 990, 1140
1960	111, 170, 277, 415, 735, 1141, 1178
1961	1, 171, 278, 348-9, 416, 1096
1962	77, 172, 225-6, 236, 242-3, 279, 350-1, 372, 520, 736, 753, 1142
1963	6, 16 (continuing), 112, 212-14, 227, 280, 417-18, 501, 991-2, 1014, 1143-5
1964	78, 113-14, 173, 244, 281, 352-4, 419, 521, 848, 993, 1146-50
1965	174, 228, 255-6, 282-3, 373, 420, 1242, 1256
1966	2, 37, 79, 115, 237, 257-8, 355, 522, 623, 849
1967	7-8, 80, 116-17, 175-6, 196-7, 421, 624, 850-3, 994-6, 1012, 1111, 1179, 1261
1968	9, 22, 119, 146, 178, 215, 229, 284, 285, 549, 559, 854-7, 997-8, 1030, 1067
1969	3, 10, 23, 179-81, 356, 523-5, 625-6, 858-60, 999, 1180-1, 1188
1970	154, 230, 259-60, 286-8, 357-9, 374, 527-8, 550-1, 627, 861-2, 927, 1068, 1234
1971	38, 81, 120-1, 147, 155, 182-3, 216, 261-3, 289, 317-18, 375-6, 422-4, 526, 628-9, 754-5, 863-4, 960, 1000, 1088, 1189, 1243-5
1972	39, 122-3, 184, 217, 264, 290-1, 360, 377-9, 529-30, 630, 738, 865-9, 951, 1069, 1112
1973	11, 82-4, 96-8, 124-6, 185-7, 218-19, 265, 292-6, 319-21, 380, 425-7, 631-4, 713, 737, 928, 948, 958-9, 1001-2, 1015, 1021, 1031, 1070, 1089, 1097, 1113, 1151, 1171-2, 1246-7
1974	85, 99-100, 127, 148-9, 156, 188-9, 238, 245, 266, 297-8, 322-3, 381-3, 473, 497, 531-2, 635, 683-4, 870-2, 943, 961, 1003-5, 1058, 1071, 1153-5, 1173, 1265
1975	128, 157, 190-2, 231, 239, 267, 299-300, 324, 361, 384, 636-8, 687-90, 873-82, 1072-3, 1090, 1114
1976	17, 86-8, 101-3, 150, 193, 240, 301-4, 362-3, 385-9, 428-9, 498-9, 533, 552, 639-40, 691-2, 883, 929-30, 1006-7, 1013, 1155, 1235

1977	18, 89-90, 129, 151-2, 194-8, 220, 305-8, 325, 364-6, 390-4, 430-1, 534-5, 641, 646, 714-16, 739-40, 1008-9, 1074
1978	4, 19, 91-2, 104, 130-2, 158, 199-200, 221, 309, 432-3, 536-7, 553, 642-3, 693, 884, 1010, 1075, 1115, 1156, 1236
1979	5, 12, 93, 133-6, 201-6, 246, 268, 310, 326-7, 395-9, 434-7, 539-40, 717, 885, 931, 1076, 1081, 1157, 1168, 1257
1980	94, 137-40, 207-8, 247-8, 311, 367, 400-01, 438-40, 476, 542, 560-61, 886, 1048, 1077, 1158, 1258-9
1981	13, 20, 95, 141, 159, 312, 368-9, 402-3, 443, 543, 644, 887-8, 932, 1011, 1116, 1159, 1169, 1237, 1248
1982	14, 142, 153, 209-10, 404-6, 474, 544, 889, 933, 1182
1983	313, 314
In press:	105-6, 143, 315, 407, 487, 554, 934, 1160, 1260

INDEX OF DISSERTATIONS

Dissertations are listed by university to which presented; all are
for the degree of Ph.D. or equivalent except where otherwise stated.

111

112

1723	1103
1729	502, 1098, 1102, 1105-6
1767	963
1770	1015, 1087
1783	see No.707(1968)
1784	1200
1791	1167
1793	509, 976
1795	463
1800	780
1801	605, 760, 1198-9, 1212
1802	1084
1803	756, 781, 815
1806	1194
1807	798, 1263
1814	1083
1815	1264
1816	457
1821	465-7, 469-70, 471, 477-9, 481, 485-8, 492, 494-5, 563, 580, 583, 590, 609, 658, 665, 668, 674-5, 678, 685, 688, 697, 699, 702, 796, 772-3, 785, 787, 790, 804, 826, 891, 945, 981, 907, 914, 1050, 1055-6
1823	444-6, 448, 451-3, 456, 459-62, 468, 578, 592, 606, 614, 647, 654, 662, 664, 669, 671, 676, 698, 765, 788, 810, 824, 829, 935, 969, 978, 1032, 1034, 1079
1826	655, 921
1827	965
1835	776
1840	556
1842	666

1849	564, 576, 615-20, 661, 677, 680, 1052, 1078
1857	1086
1859	503
1860	1238
1861	904
1865	791
1867	1082
1887	649, 656, 667, 679
1891	595
1895	768
1902	441, 489, 507, 509 (reprint), 510, 555, 565, (reprint), 573, 576 (rpt), 595 (reprint), 609 (rept), 650, 656, 675 (reprint), 677 (reprint), 685, 688, 697, 699, 702, 719, 723, 741, 744 (reprint), 747, 761, 777, 784, 785 (rpt), 816, 898, 922, 936, 940, 946, 965 (reprint), 971, 978 (reprint), 981 (rpt), 1023, 1027, 1034 (reprint) 1052 (reprint), 1055 (rpt) 1062, 1079 (reprint), 1093-4, 1099, 1107, 1121, 1174, 1192, 1195, 1203, 1215, 1222, 1239, 1252
1907	592 (reprint), 671 (rpt), 804, 969
1910	718
1916	709
1917	695, 817
1918	766, 814, 821
1926	901
1929	562, 566, 591, 600, 610, 613, 722, 767, 822, 966, 979, 982, 1183, 1214
1933	700

1935	504
1941	902, 905
1943	508, 567, 579, 653, 681, 724, 952, 972
1944	938
1947	708, 1063
1948	1122
1949	581, 596, 1078
1951	568
1955	505
1957	818
1958	557, 1121
1959	827
1965	1119, 1184-7
1966	705-6, 778, 799, 802, 1061, 1066, 1108, 1176-7
1967	450, 464, 490, 545, 547, 569-70, 574, 584, 587, 593, 597, 601, 604, 607, 611, 689, 696, 703-4, 725, 762, 769, 789, 800, 803, 807, 809, 811, 828, 892, 894, 896-7, 900, 903, 906, 908, 910-12, 916, 1024, 1064, 1100, 1120, 1121, 1193, 1196, 1201, 1204, 1213, 1216, 1253-5
1968	707, 721, 975, 1170, 1250, 1251
1969	758-9, 763-4, 770-1, 782, 793, 795, 801, 806, 808, 812, 1175
1970	1190, 1196
1971	571, 598-9, 602, 909, 955, 1217
1972	701
1973	1170
1974	694, 797, 819
1975	779, 792, 794
1977	447, 449, 458, 496, 506, 645, 686, 1240
1980	454, 472, 480, 482-4, 491, 493, 548, 572, 575, 577, 582, 585-6, 588-9, 594, 603, 608, 612, 648, 651-2, 657, 659-60, 663, 670, 672-3, 726-30, 742-3, 745-6, 748-52, 774, 783-4, 786, 805, 813, 820, 823, 893, 895, 899, 913, 915, 917-19, 920, 924-5, 937, 944, 947, 953-4, 956, 968, 970, 974, 1016-20, 1025-6, 1028-9, 1033, 1035-7, 1039-49, 1051, 1053, 1059, 1065, 1080, 1091-2, 1101, 1104, 1117, 1123-5, 1161-6, 1191, 1197, 1202, 1206-11, 1218-21, 1223-6, 1249

In press: 442, 455, 546, 825, 941, 1022, 1038, 1060, 1118

INDEX OF TRANSLATORS OF LITERARY WORKS

This Index includes translators of memoirs and of works in languages other than Russian.

INDEX OF NAMES

Underlined figures refer to main entries in Section N, "Personalia".
This Index does not include:

-editors of major collections (see pp. 103-4)
-authors of scholarly works (see pp. 109-13)
-translators of literary works (see pp. 116-17)

This Index does not include references to subjects mentioned in the titles of literary works.

Underlined figures refer to main entries in the body of the Bibliography.

ADDENDA

Abbreviations

PBRV   The Penguin Book of Russian Verse, edited by
       D. OBOLENSKY (Harmondsworth, 1962, and subsequent
       editions)

REII   The Russian Enlightenment (II), edited by D.M.
       GRIFFITHS (Canadian-American Slavic Studies, XVI, 2,
       Fall-Winter 1982)

RWEC   Russia and the West in the Eighteenth Century, edited
       by A.G. CROSS (Newtonville, Mass., 1983)

C. GENERAL HISTORIES

1266. SMITH, G.S., 'Discussant's Comments', in RWEC, 223-6.

D. LITERARY MOVEMENTS

1267. ROSENBERG, K., 'The Quarrel between Ancients and Moderns in
       Russia', in RWEC, 196-205.

See also: 1292

E. HISTORY OF IDEAS

1268. KRASINSKI, V., Sketch of the Religious History of the Slavonic
       Nations (Edinburgh, 1849).
       Pp. 292-7 discuss Freemasonry.

1269. CROSS, A.G., 'Russian Perceptions of England, and Russian
       National Awareness at the End of the Eighteenth and the
       Beginning of the Nineteenth Centuries', SEER, LXI, 1(1983),
       89-106.

1270. MADARIAGA, I.DE, 'Autocracy and Sovereignty', in REII, 369-87.

1271. BAEHR, S.L., 'In the Re-Beginning: Rebirth, Renewal and
       Renovatio in Eighteenth-Century Russia', in RWEC, 152-61.

1272. GLEASON, W., 'The Image of the West in the Journals of Mid-
       Eighteenth-Century Russia', in RWEC, 109-17.

1273. MADARIAGA, I.DE, 'Catherine and the Philosophes', in RWEC,
       30-52.

1274. RASMUSSEN, K., 'Images of National Greatness in the St.
       Petersburg and Moscow Vedomosti', in RWEC, 238-48.

See also: 1279, 1298

F. CENSORSHIP, THE PRESS

1275. JONES, W.G., 'The Polemics of the 1769 Journals: A Reappraisal', in REII, 432-43.

1276. MARKER, G., 'Discussant's Comments', in RWEC, 118-22.

See also: 1280, 1281

G. CONTACTS WITH FOREIGN LITERATURE AND CULTURE

1277. GRASSHOFF, H., 'German Awareness of Russian Literature in the Eighteenth Century', in RWEC, 20-29.

See also: 1269, 1272-4, 1285, 1292-3, 1297, 1303

I. POETRY

1278. LEVITSKY, A., 'Early Concepts of the Russian Oda dukhovnaia', in RWEC, 185-95.

K. THEATRE

See 1292

L. SPECIAL TOPICS

1279. GRIFFITHS, D.M., 'In Search of Enlightenment: Recent Soviet Interpretation of Eighteenth-Century Russian Intellectual History', in REII, 317-56.

1280. HUGHES, L.A.J., 'Architectural Books in Petrine Russia', in RWEC, 101-8.

1281. ROHLING, H., 'Illustrated Publications on Fireworks and Illuminations in Eighteenth-Century Russia', in RWEC, 94-100.

N. PERSONALIA

ANONYMOUS WORKS

Zhivopisets

1282. 'From "The Painter". Letters to Falalei', in Wiener, I, 337-41.

CATHERINE II, EMPRESS (1729-96)

Nakaz... (1767)

1283. 'The Instructions to the Commissioners for composing a New Code of Laws', translated by M. Tatishchev, in Documents of Catherine the Great. The Correspondence with Voltaire and the 'Instruction' of 1767 in the English Text of 1768, edited by W.F. REDDAWAY (Cambridge, 1931), 215-309.

1284. HYDE, G.M., The Empress Catherine and Princess Dashkov (1935)

1285. MUNRO, G.E., 'Politics, Sexuality and Servility: The Debate between Catherine II and the Abbé Chappe d'Auteroche', in RWEC, 124-34.

See also: 1273

DERZHAVIN, G.R. (1743-1816)

'Pamiatnik' (1795)

1286. 'The Monument', in PBRV, 58-9.

'Reka vremen...' (1816)

1287. 'The river of time...', in PBRV, 63.

'Solovei vo sne' (1797)

1288. 'A Nightingale in a Dream', in PBRV, 60.

'Tsyganskaia pliaska' (1805)

1289. 'The Gypsy's Dance', in PBRV, 61-2.

'Vlastiteliam i sudiiam' (1780?)

1290. 'To Rulers and Judges', in PBRV, 57-8.

KARAMZIN, N.M. (1766-1826)

1291. See No.1302

KHERASKOV, M.M. (1733-1807)

1292. GREEN, M., 'Diderot and Kheraskov: Sentimentalism in its Classicist Stage', in RWEC, 206-13.

KRYLOV, I.A. (1768-1844)

1293. CROSS, A.G., 'The English Krylov', in OSP, NS XVI(1983).

LOMONOSOV, M.V. (1711-65)

'Vechernee razmyshlenie o Bozhiem velichestve...' (1748)

1294. 'An Evening Meditation on the Divine Majesty on the Occasion of the Northern Lights', in PBRV, 52.

1295. GLEASON, W., 'The Two Faces of the Monarch: Legal and Mythical Fictions in Lomonosov's Ruler Imagery', in REII, 388-409.

1296. WEATHERSTON, R.S., 'The "Rhetoric" of Lomonosov: The Introduction and Assimilation of Modern European Communicative Models in Russia' (Ph.D., University of California, Berkeley, 1982).

NOVIKOV, N.I. (1744-1818)

1297. KEIPERT, H., 'German Writers in Novikov's Journals Utrennii svet and Moskovskoe ezhemesiachnoe izdanie (The Moralische Briefe zur Bildung des Herzens by Johann Jakob Dusch), in RWEC, 79-93.

(Novikov, N.I.)
See also: 1275

POPUGAEV, V.V. (1778-1816)

1298. RAMER, S.C., 'Vasilii Popugaev, the Free Society of Lovers of Literature, Science, and the Arts, and the Enlightenment Tradition in Russia', in REII, 491-512.

RADISHCHEV, A.N. (1749-1802)

1299. McCONNELL, A., 'Radishchev and Classical Antiquity', in REII, 469-90.

1300. PAGE, T., 'Helvetianism as Allegory in the 'Dream' and the 'Peasant Rebellion' in Radishchev's Puteshestvie iz Peterburga v Moskvu', in RWEC, 135-43.

SUMAROKOV, A.P. (1718-77)

'Pesnia' ('Tshchetno ia skryvaiu serdtsa skorbi liuty')(pub.1759)

1301. 'In vain do I hide...', in PBRV, 55.

1302. Selected Aesthetic Works of Sumarokov and Karamzin, translated and with an introduction by H.M. NEBEL, jr (Washington, D.C., 1981).

TOLSTOI, P.A. (1645-1729)

1303. OKENFUSS, M.J., 'The Cultural Transformation of Petr Tolstoi', in RWEC, 228-37.

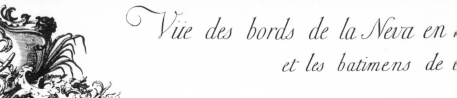

Vüe des bords de la Neva en
et les batimens de